GABRIEL'S GUIDANCE 2

More Wisdom from Archangel Gabriel

Channeled by
BEAU BUTGER

Be Love Publishing
BOYNTON BEACH, FLORIDA

Published by

Be Love Publishing

BOYNTON BEACH, FL

www.beaubutger.com

ISBN: 978-0-69289-653-2

Production by Gary A. Rosenberg
www.thebookcouple.com

Second printing 2018

Printed in the United States of America

CONTENTS

Introduction, 1

Extensions: Love, Karma, and More

INTRODUCTION

There is no "us" and "them." There is only "*all.*"

These two little sentences create one of the most powerful messages I've ever channeled. They came during the channeling sessions found in this book, and I hope they give you an idea of how incredible this book can be if you allow it.

I first began communicating with beings on other planes of existence in 2011, when I asked my angels to make their presence known by tapping me on the head three times—*and I felt their response!* Over time, I began to type messages on my computer that seemed to be coming *through* me, not *from* me, including from the Archangel Gabriel—which really threw me for a loop since I'm Jewish! But what I've learned from Gabriel is that we are all One—and that's all there is to it.

This book is confirmation that we are all One; we are all the same. All the fear and terror that is reported to us by the media is not at all what I experience in my life. There is much more peace and unity among people, at least here in the United States, than what is portrayed in the media.

I never expected to channel so much information after my first book, *Gabriel's Guidance: 101 Life Lessons from Archangel Gabriel,* was published in 2016. The topics discussed in this book are wide-ranging. For example, Gabriel repeatedly emphasizes the importance of taking 100 percent responsibility for our lives, he points out that everything is a choice, he shares universal laws, and he gives us so much wisdom to use in daily living. The channels are arranged by date rather than topic, as Archangel Gabriel and another energy who appears in these sessions, Orion, often come back to a particular lesson or topic they talked about in earlier channels. As you read this book, you'll see that not only are *we* all connected, but all this information is connected.

A word about Orion. He is an alien, or extraterrestrial. He is the most intelligent and loving being I've ever channeled.

As in my last book, my own life is sometimes used as an example to get the point of a message across. Knowing that we are all the same and that we all have the same feelings makes it a little easier for me to be OK with that. Please note that my use of "he" or "she" in a sentence is meant to imply both or either gender(s).

I can't begin to express how happy I am to share these messages with you. These messages, all these years later, continue to change my life for the better. I know they'll do the same for you. I hope you enjoy this book as much as I did when I channeled it, nearly three years ago.

Gabriel! You asked me to channel you just now. What would you like to share with me?

Gabriel: Be aware that the time has come for me to share this with you: You are the creator of every. Single. Thing. In. Your. Life. Every up. Every down. Every sacrifice. Everything that is taken away from you and everything that is given to you is your calling. You are bringing everything in your life into your life. Do you get that? You bring it all.

Things happen, and you bring those situations into your life. For example, if there was an accident on the freeway and you were on the freeway at the time of that accident, you brought yourself to it. You knew deep inside that there was going to be that accident. Your thoughts create your life. If you are down, then you bring in those situations that are negative or not in alignment with a spontaneously incredible life. Same thing goes if you are in a great mood. When you are in a great mood, the things that show up are happy. They are contagious and fun to experience. Love the life you live. It is all up to you. I really want you to get this positive, incredible space of love that I am sharing with you.

(I find this to be absolutely nuts sometimes. Why would we attract negative situations to ourselves? Well, it's the same idea as attracting positive situations. We attract what we think and what we feel. It seems what we feel is more important in this situation.)

I didn't expect to be told that at all. So, we are literally the creators of our own life? I guess that would make sense if we are God in human form.

Gabriel: I'm glad you are able to appreciate the life you are given and understand how it is working. The Universe is the genie in your bottle. Rub it the right way and your dreams come true. Rub it the wrong way and suffer the consequences. This is not meant to sound evil. However, I do want you to understand this and really accept the impact of it all. You are literally creating your entire life, moment by moment. I've shared this before and I really want you to get this, for this is so important. The God in you is you. Wow! Do you get this?

(That *is powerful and a reminder that we are God in human form!*)

The God *in* me *is* me? I understand the concept, but please explain this in more detail for me.

Gabriel: You are God. It is that simple. God is you. You are God. Here we go again! You are creating all of this life that you live. You start from the top and work your way to the bottom. From beginning to end is your creation. Boom—done. All there is is love and life and your thoughts. That's it.

(*Doesn't that sentence explain it all? "All there is is love and life and your thoughts." I feel we would all benefit greatly if we reminded ourselves of this as often as possible.*)

Well, if we are creating every moment of our lives, then how does the life lesson *God helps those who help themselves* fit in? Aren't *we* technically creating those situations that help move us along on our journey? Do you know what I mean by this?

Gabriel: Oh yes, I do. Remember, Beau, *you are God in human form*. There is you and only you. You build and destroy. It's really that easy. Humans complicate life. It's really not that difficult. Your current society has grown [in such a way as to make it] hard to understand each other. The spirit world, for the most part, has become spooky and hard to believe. There is nothing to fear in any of this. I love you.

The Aztecs fully understood all of this. The comprehension that pertains to the value of life is the moment you realize that everything about you is the greater God within. The cherished lives of others are created by them and them alone.

This is all boiling down to "We create our own lives. Everything." This was talked about already. I'm curious why you're sharing this.

Gabriel: If you look at your life right now, and the book you are about to begin reading in which the first chapter is called "Take 100% Responsibility for Your Life," then realize that it all relates to you.

To me? Shouldn't this relate to everyone and not just me?

Gabriel: Oh, but it does—for you are everyone and everything. You are all One. We are all One!

(We are God/the Universe in human form. We create everything in our lives. It is in us. This is why taking 100 percent responsibility for our life is an important choice to make. It makes us fully responsible. We then let the Universe or angels do the rest.)

We definitely are. So does that mean that all of the life lessons that were previously shared, which were explained using examples from my own life, are things that everyone is going or has gone through?

Gabriel: In their own way, yes. You can all relate to one other. *You,* as in human beings. You all go through the same ups and downs, and yet because you believe in different things—whether it's spirituality, religion, or nothing at all; plus the color of your skin—you end up dividing yourself. Why? There is no need to do this. There is one God. You are God. The God of life is you. God is everything. Did you already forget this?

(We are all the same. We chose to divide and think we're different because of religion and race.)

I didn't think I did. I understand why you say that, though. I feel like you're really talking to everyone who will read this.

Gabriel: That is *exactly* what I'm doing.

I get it. Is that everything you wanted to share in regard to you asking me to channel you?

Gabriel: Continue living life and knowing you are the creator of all of this. The life you live is created by you and *only* you. There is no "us" and "them." There is only "*all.*"

(There are times in these channelings that I'm taken aback by certain messages. This is one of them.)

That is powerful! Wow! All right. Gabriel, *thank you* for sharing all of this. I love you! Till next time?

Gabriel: Till next time.

Hi, Gabriel! I saw myself in space just now. Orion showed up in his spaceship and told me to plant my feet into the two stars below me. I did that, channeled you, and then channeled Orion. That was amazing! Can you please confirm all of that?

> **Orion:** The vast universe is filled with truth and perfection that can never be eliminated by human existentialism. The planet Earth is a speck in the vastness that you call the Universe. God is the Universe. God is everything, as Gabriel has told you. Know that the chapter for a new expansion starts now, and I am the one asked to lead you. Gabriel is here with me, and we will be the ones that speak to you from here on out for this new book. This book of ascension will be labeled correctly and clearly, for there are no mistakes in the celebration of life. I am here to guide you into the best life you can ever live, plus more, and Gabriel will assist me in this as well.
>
> I, Orion, am the celebration of life as what you call an alien. The new moon has come and gone, and now you are here to enjoy the ride from here on out. I will be guiding you up and down through the experiences that life offers. You will be taught a new experience that can only be truly accepted if you open your heart to it. The best way I can explain this expansion is: Be brilliant every day in every aspect of life, for there is only love at the end of it. *Heaven,* as some of you call it, is just another form of love. Love is the same aspect of life. Life is love and love is life.

(A new communicator! What incredible words. Am I the only one who feels that beings from other planets and galaxies are far more advanced than we are?)

I was taught by Gabriel that God is love, and I also think I was told that God is life. You also just said that God is everything, which would make sense if God is love *and* life. God is literally *everything*.

> **Orion:** Good, Beau. Keep getting this. If God is everything and you are everything and everything is everything, that would make you God in human form. I am God in "alien" form. Do you get this? This is the biggest lesson for you to get in this life. God is you. You are God. God is God is God is God is God. There are no mistakes, for the ascension for human beings is being formed right now through the creative consciousness. The planet is in alignment with a change that has been waiting to happen for a long time. The planet is a living creature. Treat it as such.

(Let's treat this planet with respect, for it is alive.)

I never really looked it at like that. I know plants are living beings, but I never saw the actual planet as that.

> **Gabriel:** Hi, Beau! This is Gabriel. Everything is on the right path for you to get all of this and share with the world. The changes being made to your brain patterns are the changes that are happening to the planet. It's the same idea. The existence of man is created by man. I know. That's deep.

What in the world do you mean by that, Gabriel? Our existence is created by *us*? Where does God come into all of this?

> **Gabriel:** You are taking that too literally. What I mean by this is that the way you live your lives is created by you. God is not up there pointing down and saying, "OK, do this. Now do that. Do this. Do that." That's not how life goes. God assists when the time is right for things to come to fruition on the planet, and God is not leading anyone to do anything specific in this life. Everything can be conquered by you and you alone. There is vastness in this universe that can only be appreciated when you sit back and really allow yourself to take it all in.

I'm doing my best not to have all of my responses be "Wow!" but . . . *wow!* This is incredible stuff to be told. I thought the vastness was so big that our human brains could never fully understand it.

(Think about what infinity looks like. Go ahead. I'll wait.)

> **Orion:** I want you to understand that the complexity of the Universe is so much larger than even I sometimes understand. There is infinity. Humans don't understand the idea of infinity but know that infinity *does* exist. It's hard to understand even for us, but know that it does in fact exist. I want you to take what I'm about to say into consideration.

(If beings of a higher intelligence have trouble fully grasping what infinity looks like, then it is, in my opinion, absolutely impossible for humans to get it.)

I was just typing something that made *no* sense at all, so I stopped simply because I thought I was making it up. Gabriel, I'm curious why I'm channeling you *and* Orion. Can one of you please explain this? I am confused, considering I was only channeling Archangel Gabriel for the last book. Are we even going to stick to life lessons?

> **Gabriel:** Absolutely—and even more than that. I brought Orion into this conversation because there are things that are best described by Orion. Orion is an intergalactic transformational being who watches over the planet and universe. Orion does things that I as an archangel am not here to accomplish. There are also aspects of the universe that are better understood by Orion. Orion, please explain further for Beau.

> **Orion:** The transformative aspect of life that I will share with you is just the ribbon in the fine interwoven experience of life as you know it. God is the one that forms all. All is God. Understand that the vast universe that you understand is only partial, for there are galaxies that I've traveled to that the human race may never fully grasp. That's fine. You don't have to know everything.

Don't take that too literally! But when you are told that God is everything, which makes you everything—you *can* take that literally. You don't have to understand God fully, for you really cannot do this. Nor do you have to understand yourself fully, for there are things about you that will never fully be understood in the life you live. You will "get" many things, and there are teachers like you and others who will express ways of life that make a difference for you.

However, the human race does not fully have to understand itself. That's why we are here. That's why books such as this are made. We help to have you be the best you that you can be. Love life. Live love. Love love. Love conquers all. Love is all there is, Beau. That's it.

I can see you're touched and moved by this. *Love is love is love is love is love.* Love everything and everybody. Love *yourself*. This is *so* important for you to get. *Love yourself.* When you love yourself, you love everybody and everything else, for you are all connected. We are connected. Believe.

(Please allow yourself to read that again if need be. That was a lot *of information.)*

This is a *lot* to take in. I really don't even know where to go from here, for I don't want just to ask you what the next life lesson is. This is a new book that is supposed to be filled with new information. I feel the need to end this conversation. I am overwhelmed right now. Thank you, Gabriel and Orion. What a journey this will be.

Orion: The new journey you are on will open you and everyone else up to a new life that is meant for you to finally experience. Those who will get it will get it. That's really all there is to it.

Wow. That's all I can say.

Did I just channel Archangel Gabriel and Orion?

Gabriel: Yes!

Orion: Yes, you did, Beau. This is Orion. I love you. Don't ever be afraid of me.

Well, OK. I'm still really unfamiliar with this new scene—channeling you two beings in space and grounding myself in stars. It really feels genuine.

Orion: Don't worry, for you are entitled to your own feelings. This is the way the world works even when it doesn't seem to be going according to plan. The main thing I want you to get is that this is all a dream you are experiencing, for this is made up. I am not saying that this channeling is a dream, but life itself is a dream. Dreams show up and dreams go away. Life shows up and life goes away. There is a very specific discipline that must be accomplished for you to win at this game of dreams.

The game for you to consider experiencing is the one where you win. Winning is awesome. Losing is even better because it's in losing that you really find your true calling. The loss of someone is similar, meaning that the loss of a loved one truly defines who you are at your core. How you handle yourself. The mourning process is just that. It is a process. You always remember *and* you learn to live without. You learn to live without for a lot of things.

Orion, who is me, is here to show you the way to live your most epic life. I am here to accomplish a way of being that you never really took into consideration and also to accomplish an alignment with the greatest self that you can be. The cherished life of the souls that inhabit this earth is destined to be superior in all areas of life, and at the same time . . . life is a choice. You may do what you want with it. No one and no thing is leading the way for you. You are here to serve one purpose, and that is to be the experience of God. God is God is God is God is God.

(Life is a dream? If I take into consideration that things I think about and want to manifest happen, then that makes sense. To know that we can daydream a new reality for ourselves, work toward it, and then have it happen makes this reality's being a dream believable. We dream deeper at those moments than the dream we live in.)

Life is a dream? I'm really stuck on that one. Please explain further what you mean by "Life is a dream." All there is is love and life and your thoughts.

Gabriel: I want you to believe you are destined for greatness. Now, greatness is different for everyone. Be the best you that you can be! Cherish your life and life will cherish you back. Life *always* cherishes you, actually.

Orion: I want you to consider that your awake state is a dream and your dream state is truly just clues for your dream. The other side is the real you. You know this. You believe that. You are here for a short time with missions to fulfill, and everyone forever has a different mission. No two are exactly the same. Some want this and some want that and some are supposed to do this and some are supposed to do that. Don't get caught up in the *how*. Get caught up in the *Now. Now* is all there is, Beau. That's it. Nothing more. Nothing less.

I love that. Don't get caught up in the how; get caught up in the *Now!* That's amazing! In other words, don't worry about *how* it'll happen. Enjoy what's happening at that moment. Enjoy the journey. Be yourself. Don't take things personally. The journey may not look like how you thought. You'll get to where you're supposed to be. Am I getting it? I'm taking everything I learned from the last book with Archangel Gabriel. Am I right about everything?

Orion: "Right" is a choice. Remember what Archangel Gabriel said: "There is no 'right' and there is no 'wrong'." It's whatever you choose to make it mean. Things happen. Life happens. Love it or leave it.

Right. Orion, you mentioned that it takes a specific discipline to win at this dream. What am I out to win?

Orion: You win whatever you want to win, and again, it may not look how you expected it to look. Do dreams ever make complete sense when they're happening? No, yet they end up making complete sense the more you think about it. Look at life like that. Ponder that you accomplish everything you want regardless of how you're feeling. If you feel that you aren't worth it, then that is the kind of life you will accomplish. Your feelings determine the kind of life that you live. The generous gift that we have been given by God is the underlying premise that we are in control of everything. You are the Universe in human form. You bring yourself to . . . yourself. You are bringing the Universe to yourself. Therefore, you are bringing life to yourself. Therefore, you are bringing experiences to yourself. Therefore, you are bringing everything to yourself.

Life is not fair only when you decide in your mind that it's not fair. Everything is a choice. Literally. You dream your life, Beau. You make all of it up. That's why Archangel Gabriel said that you do everything to yourself. You are in control and creating it as you go along. Now you can create ahead of time and watch things unfold, and it is truly up to you how things go as you get to where you want to be. Do you follow? You choose everything. There is no "meant to be" when you are in control. At the same time, there is a "meant to be" when you choose a certain outcome.

(You are in control of your life. Nobody and nothing else is. What if you took on the challenge for a day of not questioning what happens and took complete responsibility for your life?)

That practically answered the question I've had for a while about how things are meant to be *only* based on the path that we chose to take. That's so fascinating. You also said that we really only have one purpose, and that is to be the "experience of God." I know that God experiences life through us. Are you saying that we are really only here for God to experience life? We are God in human form. We create everything. We decide, dream, and write down the life we want. I'm still confused, though, where God exists in all this.

Gabriel: God is everything.

Orion: Well, take into consideration that since God is everything and you *are* God, you are the only one who determines your life. You see, people think God is in charge and decides who comes, who goes, who experiences what, who chooses everything. That's not how it works. *You and only you* are in charge of life and of your life. You as a global community decide what shows up. Really. That's all there is to it. The global community right now is begging for what you are typing to come to the Earth.

So we as a global community are also deciding upon wars and bloodshed?

Orion: Yes, you are. Does that make sense to you? Probably not. There is a strong enough coordination that causes certain extremes to happen.

This is so hard to take in and believe. Why would we choose war and bloodshed?

Orion: You are only human, and you are not convinced yet that you are all One.

(I'm convinced now! We as a global community would exist so much better in peace and love.)

It's that simple, huh?

> **Gabriel:** Yes! The life you live is a choice. The life you live is a choice made by you, and then everyone around you feeds into it. There is a point at which you can decide to change it. Now, this doesn't mean that if you're crippled, you can all of a sudden walk. At the same time, this has happened. It's a belief so strong that words cannot truly explain it. Accidents happen. People fight for these [accidents and diseases] to go away. Those who believe and work and fight tooth and nail will change their life forever. Some things people are born with and want to experience from a soul purpose.

I am *so* confused! *If* we can change the things that happen to us but we can't change things we're *born* with . . . I don't even know where I'm going with that. In my head, it makes sense, but I'm having trouble putting it on paper. There are things that our soul chose to experience and be born with, and we can decide if we want to work around them or not. There are things that happen later in life that have the same meaning. There are also things we didn't choose to happen before we came here, and we can fight those things off?

> **Orion:** You're on the right track but not quite there.

So, can you please explain in more detail?

> **Orion:** The life that you choose is determined by you. Take into consideration that "you" isn't the human you. It's you as a soul. As a spirit. As the astral being that you are. You bring everything to yourself. You are the planet in human form. You are the Universe in human form. You are God in human form. We are *all* connected. You choose. We choose. We all choose each other's life!

My brain can't seem to wrap itself around any of that. There's only so much I can take!

(This is still a lot to take in, reading this nearly two years later!)

> **Gabriel:** Life cannot be put into a book. Humans will never really understand life fully, and it's designed to be that way. I love you.

I love you, too, Gabriel. I love you as well, Orion. I am ready to unchannel. I can't think straight anymore—ha! Bye!

> **Orion:** Until next time. Love is always around you. *Always.*

Hi, Gabriel! Hi, Orion! It's great to channel you two.

Orion: Know that the transmutation of your mind is beginning to take place at this exact moment. The time has come for you to move on to a new conversation about the planets and galaxies that you weren't quite prepared for during our last conversation. Know that the moment you realize that we are all One is the moment you realize that everything around you—the planets, the stars, the moon, and even the wallet on your desk that you're looking at—is One. The water, the trees, the bees, and the fish. You and we are all One.

We're all connected, huh? I feel like I'm at a point where I don't doubt.

Gabriel: Know that the time has come for you to realize that everything we have told you up until this point is barely even the tip of the iceberg, for there is so much for you to learn about how this universe works and operates. God is so beyond anything that you understand. The temperature in your mind is rising, for you are about to experience an explosion of heat rays! Obviously, this is metaphorically speaking. Don't worry!

(I definitely don't want my head on fire!)

Thank goodness! So, what can you tell me?

Orion: What I can tell you is that there is a star count in this universe that is a larger number than humans have yet to grasp. The vastness of this universe is beyond anything you can truly fathom, for there are multi-levels of universes within *this* universe. You will never understand it, and that is OK, for you really don't have to understand it to experience it or think about it. There is so much going on in the universe right now, at this exact moment, that your brain is literally incapable of being able to describe it. This doesn't make you stupid at all. There is just too much going on. Also, there are multi-levels to the dimensions and strings of galaxies and ideas that are hard to fathom. There are different versions of you, and even different versions of pets, and you are inhabiting one of those versions right now. There is a galaxy version of you that has three arms and forty-five legs. I know. You don't have to believe that at all. Just know that whatever your mind can imagine exists at some level. I love you. This is Orion.

(I have trouble keeping a good balance with two legs!)

Three arms and forty-five legs? Did I type that right?

Orion: Yeah, you did. There are no accidents, Beau.

OK. I won't lie. That is *very* hard to imagine—and *why* would a version of me like that even exist? Why in the world would I need forty-five legs?!

Orion: Oh, but why wouldn't you need those legs? You see, there are galaxies and planets and other such things that you won't be able to wrap your head around. This is going to get way out there. Be prepared not to believe a lot of this.

(Let me know if you believe some of this stuff, because this gets weird. Even I had a hard time believing a lot of this when I originally channeled it, and I believe everything that comes through these channels.)

We're already heading down that road, I see. I know I need to trust what comes in, but that is extremely hard to wrap my head around. Forty-five legs. Three arms. Let's move on to something else. What else can you share with me?

Orion: Did you know that the version of yourself you want to become already exists in another dimension? String theory—does that ring a bell? The existence of you in a new body living the life you'd rather be living exists. You see, you can switch into that new version of you whenever you'd like. Do you remember when Gabriel taught you the lesson about the butterfly, and how you are One?

(This is a reference to my first book channeling Archangel Gabriel, called Gabriel's Guidance.)

Yes, I do. Are you saying that it's like that? It's like I'm a caterpillar morphing into a butterfly? When I'm ready to do something new in my life, I turn from a caterpillar into a butterfly? For instance, if I am not in shape and I decide to start working out, then the new me that is in shape and healthy is the new butterfly version of me?

Gabriel: You're getting it! I'm so proud of you, Beau. There is so much for you to get in this life. I love you! Keep listening to Orion, for Orion is brilliant beyond the stars. You have never met anyone or anything as intelligent as Orion!

(We can move from one dimension to another instantly. We can move from one version of ourselves to another instantly. That's absolutely incredible to think about. I personally feel we switch moment to moment since we make plans to do things and don't always follow through with them for one reason or another. This is such a great idea to be reminded of two years later, though.)

Not even you?

Gabriel: It's a different kind of amicable sponsorship of love.

I don't even know what that means, but . . . OK. I'll take your word on that! So, there's a version of me out there in another dimension that has everything I'm striving for? Wow!

Orion: Trust me. You exist. You don't understand you exist, and so you never take a walk in those shoes. Once you take a walk in those shoes and see what life looks like in that dimension as that version of you, you'll *never* want to come back and visit this one. This version of you is beautiful and perfect. That version of you is also beautiful and perfect. It's your free-will choices that decide if that's where you will live or if you choose to live here or in another dimension.

Life is a parallelogram of universal magic that captures the very essence of your being. Love is love is love is love is love. Love yourself, Beau. Trust yourself. Don't be afraid of *anything*. Conquer life. Be stupendous. Only you can decide how your life goes. It's up to you to travel to different dimensions and take on those other versions of you. Did you know there's a version of you out there that is strung out on cocaine? It's a scary and miserable life that you're leading. The version of you that is channeling me has kept himself from that kind of life, and your actions and intelligence will never let you get there. Isn't that remarkable?

That really is. Is there also a version of me out there that follows through on decisions he makes and has common sense? Ha!

Orion: Yes. Absolutely. Whatever you can imagine of yourself exists out there. God lives through your decisions. There are endless versions of you and of the planet so God can understand how it is to be a certain way as each person. God is existing *as* life to experience life.

Wow, that's deep. Is there anything else you'd like to share with me regarding all of this?

Orion: The only thing that you need to know is that you are in control and you can visit those different versions of yourself whenever you decide to do so. There is *nothing* stopping you or getting in your way except you. That's it. Be yourself. Be you. Be gentle but be unstoppable, especially in the face of no agreement. Love. Conquer. Love.

This is so much to take in, Orion. I need a break!

Orion: And do just that.

Thank you, Orion. Thank you, Gabriel. Gabriel, is there any last message that you would like to leave me with before I go?

Gabriel: Be acceptance! Be you. Be beautiful.

Gracious and glorious as always. Thank you, Gabriel. Till next time!

Hello, Gabriel and Orion! How are you two?

> **Orion:** You are one of the souls that has come here to open up the gates of love and happiness and peace and to show the world you are all One and the same. We are all One. Me, you, God, water, land, her, him, it, them, us. It's all One eternal being of love and courage.

How can I start to help?

> **Gabriel:** Beau, be yourself. You are love and light in human form, and there is more to you than just love and light, for you are eternal.

(I am no more special than anyone else. Be yourself, for you can use your talents to help make this world a better place. Don't wait until your mid-thirties to start. Start now because this world can really use it right now and always.)

Aren't *all* human beings eternal? Especially if we're all One and come from the same place. Am I right about this?

> **Orion:** Orion here. You are right, for the changes you will see on the planet will be started to move the unit *(presence)* of love, and your message is one of the many that will help move it forward. The changes that are coming to this planet are grand, and you are helping, as well as thousands of others. Love and light surround you. The light beings that you work with will help you along the way by giving you information to download into your subconscious field. The love of the light beings is strong. Trust you are safe at these times, and watched over, for you have things that must be done. You are in fact on a mission; your humanness

won't let you understand that, and that is fine. Be safe. Take care of yourself.

What lessons about life or other galaxies or this universe can you share with me tonight?

Gabriel: The giant aura that you all possess is more than just an aura, a light. Beau, you are the galaxy in human form, and therefore, if you take that into consideration, then all the germs that surround you are alive. They are alive and living and hovering on the planet of you. The galaxy of you. The universe of you. God is clever beyond your world and realm of existence.

That's a fascinating way to look at it. Please go into further detail. I imagine that is something Orion will talk about.

Orion: Beau, you are right. This is Orion. The light beings that you are working with are intergalactic light beings from other dimensions, and they are like the germs of the universe. I want you to understand this better. Think about that. The universe is combined of many different galaxies and dimensions that you are not able to see. You cannot see the germs that surround you, but they are there. The world as you know it is not the world you think it is.

The energy that exists on this planet is beyond the comprehension of humankind, and that does not make you stupid, dumb. You are infinitely intelligent beings, but you do not allow yourselves to be that. You have it in you, Beau. You are all geniuses and don't see it. You put limits on yourselves. Stop wasting your life away, humankind. You are all much bigger and smarter than that. Go after what you love, for that is what you are meant to do. Do you realize that the gifts you were each individually given are what makes the planet better? The love that exudes out of your love cell is more than you have ever imagined.

Love cell? Do you mean aura?

Orion: Yes, I do.

(By cell, I mean a holding cell and not a cell in your body. Also, we as humans are so intelligent, but we don't give ourselves enough credit. What if we all lived life knowing we are brilliant and that we can create anything? I really think that would elevate us as a species.)

I know we haven't been communicating that long tonight, but I am going to end it here. I will channel again very soon to continue this conversation.

Orion: Beau. One more thing. The love of your life is right beside you, and you don't even realize it.

Do you mean the person who's the love of my life romantically?

Orion: Yes, I do. The future is around you. This is something human beings don't really get. When you are living the life you are, you are creating it moment by moment, and so you are living in the life you are creating. It is around you. You just have to open up your eyes and yourself to see it. You are on the right track, and I want you to even go deeper than that. Sleep on it. I love you. This is Orion. We can go into more detail about this in our next conversation.

OK. That's so fascinating. Thank you. I love you.

Orion: And we love you, Beau.

Hi, Gabriel! How are you?

> **Gabriel:** I should be asking you that same question. You've gone over two months without channeling on your own. The time flies. Please make the effort to do this on a regular basis. Eat healthier.

Please explain in more detail what you mean by "Eat healthier."

> **Gabriel:** I can do that. Always listen to your stomach. Always listen to your energy path. Always listen to your instincts. One of the biggest lessons for you to gather during this adventure is to make your own decisions. This goes back to the lesson that was shared with you about being self-reliant. Learn to trust yourself. This goes for much more than just food. This goes for everything that you are accomplishing.

(It is the beginning of 2017 as I write this, and I am just now starting not to let what others think about me affect me. You will have ideas throughout your life, but you might not start putting them into action for a few years, and that's OK. You can begin whenever you're ready. The Universe will wait for you, and it will always *be on your side.)*

> **Gabriel:** Trust your gut. If it feels right, then keep going. If not, then stop. Trust your instincts. That was one of the first lessons I taught you, Beau. Follow up with yourself regarding these lessons.

Why can't most of the messages I've been receiving recently be clearer?

> **Gabriel:** Do you remember what Karen said, that you needed to be taught that those thoughts aren't your normal brain patterns?

(Karen is a family friend who also channels Archangel Gabriel. What are the chances?!)

Yeah.

Gabriel: OK, good. So now that you've made that request to be more clear, Orion and I will be more clear in our communication. This also comes back to these conversations. Trust what is coming out. The words I share with you are not from your thoughts. As your mom has pointed out to you on a number of occasions, this is not your voice. It's mine!

(Archangel Gabriel has always been silly and so lighthearted.)

Ha! What a lovely sense of humor you have, Gabriel. OK, so now that we have all that out of the way, what would you like to share with me during this channeling? Are we going back to life lessons?

Gabriel: Let's pass on the life lessons for now. We will come back to that. Call in Orion please.

Orion: Hi. This is Orion speaking. The gift of life was created for the upliftment of God itself. The unique perspectives you each have as individuals is the pure essence of life as you know it. The following explanation is not my words. This is from a higher source of intelligence:

The light upon you is now full circle upon the horizon of the gods. Trust the words I share. The universe was once a kaleidoscope of wonder. The world you now live in is the creation of the higher being that you call God. There is just so much more to that than you can comprehend right now. The world is the turnip for the vegetable garden of life. The world is love. You are the world and God and everything of the universe, in the form of a human element. The foundation of life is to help expand God even larger than God already is— and God is infinite. How do you stretch infinite, you ask? Easy. You choose. You decide to expand, and so it is. You as humans choose to kill, and so it is. The majority of human beings are the pinnacle of perfection and have never understood the concept, and so they are all treating each other as meat. That's not what this is about. Free will has gotten in the way of your light. Be One with each other and know you are a heavenly elegance on the planet Earth.

I'm speechless. Where do I go from here? I don't even know if I can explain that in simpler terms.

(Let me try, though. This energy is saying that we may not understand this because we as humans can't wrap our head around what is truly happening, not only on the planet but in the universe. A grace is coming to our planet, though. I am clear we are at the beginning of a new age of life on earth. We are God/the Universe in human form, which makes us all the same and all One. Why are we killing each other? If the world is love, then we are love. It's my understanding we are here to give experience of life and what it's like to God/the Universe/whatever you choose to call it.)

Orion: You don't have to. Those who are supposed to get it will do just that. I love you.

Orion, who did those words come from?

Orion: There is no name for this being.

Is this being even larger and more powerful than what we humans call God?

Orion: Who said it wasn't?

Touché. I guess just because it mentioned God in third person doesn't mean that wasn't God. Then again, God is everything.

Orion: I am smiling through you. You're getting it. Even if that isn't the God you understand, everything is connected. Everything is "all."

I am going to unchannel because there is only so much I can take. Ha!

Orion: Be with these thoughts. I love you.

Bye, Orion. Till next time, Gabriel!

Gabriel: Bye!

Hi, Gabriel! Did I receive your message correctly just now?

Gabriel: The documentation you are about to receive is correct and something you should follow closely. Follow my lead. Be the personal trainer of your own movement for the next two weeks. Channeling me will bring you not only closer to God, but closer to me. It will bring you more joy, peace, and longevity on this spiritual journey. The everlasting essence of your being lies within these lessons that I share with you. I'm not going anywhere. Be with me on this journey, and your spirit will open up to receive new advantages to be with your higher Self.

I know that you are down, and that's OK. Remember, as you've realized (and your mom has realized), things must get worse before they get better. Be with this. Know that any aggravation, any changes you are going through emotionally, and everything you are experiencing is part of this process. It is also the change in your Earth age that has brought a new clarity to certain events in your life.

(Regarding my earth age, my birthday is May 16. Now that you know, I'll be expecting a card in the mail. Ha!)

Wow, Gabriel! That sounds mighty important! It *does* sound biblical, but I know that's not how it's meant. What else would you like to share about what you just mentioned?

Gabriel: The being that you are is expanding to receive something you have not yet received. I mean by this that you are just becoming ready to be the person you always wanted to become— and more. Your whole being, as well as your mind, is being used to bring peace and love to the planet.

Wow, Gabriel! Would you like me to call Orion in for this channeling, or is this just me and you this time?

Gabriel: The element of surprise is a wonderful element! Be the aura seeker!

I don't even know what that means. What do you mean by *aura seeker?*

Gabriel: To put it in words you may better understand, the essence of your being is to help create logic amongst those who do not yet get that we are all connected. The being of the world is short-lived, and you are all here to expand it. Channel Orion now so Orion can expand on this lesson.

Orion: The elements that run through the solar system have come here to meet each other and help expand the planet. The essence of love is here to be broadcast throughout the world, and your generation as well as others after it are here to bring love and peace to the planet. Things may not look like they are getting better, but they are. Trust us. They are. Love is all there is, and the new generation of Earth angels is understanding this very clearly. They are getting that there is no separation between anyone.

They don't understand the hatred and separation that continues amongst older generations. They are here to understand that we and you are all One. There is no "them" and no "us." There is only "all." This is a lesson that was pointed out to you in a previous channeling. Know that every message we give you all comes back to the same two things: 1) We are all connected, and 2) We are all Love. It is a form of love that you will never quite get as human beings—and that is OK. The love you understand currently is more than enough. The beings that you are, are here forever. There is no going anywhere.

You are wondering what I mean by this. Let me explain that for you. By "being," I don't necessarily mean "human being," for your true essence is much more than that. You are a soul. A spirit. A light being. The light you are, which is God, is here forever. God is infinite. If you are part of God, then that makes you infinite. You are love. You are all connected, and you are part of God. That is beautiful to think about, isn't it?

I almost began to tear up, Orion! That is beautiful to think about! What a gift you have given me and readers! Thank you! What else would you like to share?

Orion: Oh, there is so much more that you will learn over the next two weeks as you channel Gabriel and me every day. I know your mom will love that. Be aware that we have some catching up to do, Beau. This is another reason we are asking you to channel us every day for the next two weeks. Set a reminder. Write notes. After you eat your breakfast, channel us. Get it done first thing in the morning. That way, you don't have to think about it the rest of the day. The time is here. The time is now. The expansion is upon us!

(I can't believe I went so long without channeling! The lesson here: Don't procrastinate.)

Oh. My. God . . . . Where do I go from here?

Orion: You channel Gabriel.

Gabriel: Hi Beau! It's Gabriel! Picture me waving at you frantically! OK, here's the deal: We are going to end this channeling tonight. Starting tomorrow will be the first day of the rest of your lives.

I think I know what you mean by "our lives," but let me just make sure. Does "our lives" mean everyone on the planet's lives? Not just mine?

Gabriel: Yes! Now go! Enjoy your night! I love you!

I love you, too, Gabriel and Orion!

Hi Gabriel! Hi Orion! Good morning. So today and for the next two weeks, you want me to channel you two so you can share a lot of important information, right?

Gabriel: Yes! We are here to expand further upon the life lessons and more so the planet and everything that is going on with you and the world. The planet is in need of some compassion and love, and you are one of the thousands that is here to bring light to the world through your channeling of me. There are about as many people as well that can channel Orion, so you are not as special as you thought! Ha! I'm just kidding! I love you! You, as well as everyone else on this planet, are special.

(I believe a large number of people on earth now are here to bring light to it. We are in a new age, and there are more people on this planet now than ever before.)

Gabriel: Eat your greens, everyone! Clarity of the mind comes in the form of healthy natural eating. Organic for your organs!

Ha! Why did you just share that last sentence? What does that have to do with anything you are about to have me write?

Gabriel: Everyone thinks that there is no difference (for the most part) between organic and nonorganic. This is more so for the nonbelievers of it. I am not here to judge, for there is nothing to judge. I am simply here to pass on information to you and the planet. There is a big difference between GMO and non-GMO. The difference is simple: GMOs are not good for your soul, spirit, or your being. The contradiction of life is set forth in the polarity of your scanning brain.

(I didn't realize this was going to become a lesson on food.)

Please be clearer for me. What do you mean by this?

> **Gabriel:** The longevity of your soul, spirit, and being lies in how you treat them. Bad foods are like bad thoughts. Bad thoughts eat away at your core and your health emotionally, spiritually, and physically. Bad foods also eat away at your core and your health, emotionally, spiritually, and physically. There is a connection to everything.
>
> Look at it like this. GMO can be used as an abbreviation for God Must Obey. If you put bad foods into your system, then that is a choice, right? Life is a choice. Therefore, what you put into your body is a choice. We as angels will try to guide you away from poor choices, but ultimately, you have free will and can do what you please. So, GMO = God Must Obey. This means that if you choose to put GMOs into your body, then God Must Obey that. God obeys you.
>
> Let's get more technical here. If life is a choice and you have free will, you can do whatever you want. God does not interfere with any of the choices you make. God may and does show up to point you in the direction that will lead you to be your best you, but again, it is your choice which path you choose to get to where you want to be. There is no "Do this now or you will go to hell!" There is no hell, for the devil is a fairytale and made up by human beings to scare you and put fear into your hearts. There is no such thing.
>
> I am not here to say there is not any dark energy. For every yin, there is a yang. What I am saying is that there is no devil, nor is there a hell. There is no fiery pit. What there is, is self-aggravation, self-torture, and self-torment. Do you see where I am going with this? You do everything to yourself.

(Wow! That was basically a long and interesting way of saying that our free will "gets in the way." Our free will lets us make poor choices throughout our life. That's deep.)

Whoa, that was *heavy!* God Must Obey. That's a fascinating acronym. I felt one coming, and I couldn't figure out what you were going to say. It's a bit abstract without a solid explanation. What else would you like to share?

> **Orion:** The time has come for me to share with you that the world is going to explode with love and peace and harmony, and it will be in your lifetime, Beau. Isn't that great? The world is healing. It is ending its Dark Ages, so to speak. The love that you talk about in your songs and that is talked about in so many channelings you've done, as well as many other offerings by God, is finally happening. Things had to get worse before they got better.
>
> As your mom said, everyone doesn't go through that, and therefore it is not a universal law. I want you to understand that the being you are becoming is the essence of this love. You are love. We are love. Everyone and everything is love. Some people just don't realize it yet. Some never will in their earth life and that's OK. They will get it when they return home.

> **Gabriel:** This is Gabriel. Remember that everything we tell you has a foundation of love, so literally everything is love. Even our words. How fun is that?

You two are crazy. Ha! Everything is love. I got it and already understood that through past lessons throughout my spiritual journey. It's always nice to be reminded, though. Is there anything you'd like to share with me this morning?

> **Orion:** Be courageous! This is not just for you, Beau. This is for everyone. Remember the Maya Angelou quote that you read yesterday? If there is no courage, then there is nothing. You must

have courage to do anything. Life takes courage. Love takes courage. Courage, courage, courage! Causing Overall Unity Released Amongst God's Energy.

Does that acronym even make sense? I feel like I made that up.

Orion: Keep looking at it to figure it out, because there is truth in those words. Did you make it up? Well, are you making any of this up?

(I used to wonder that when I began channeling.)

Sometimes I wonder, though I know I'm not. There are two different voices coming through me. It's obvious to me.

Orion: OK, good. Now that you realize that you did not make it up, take into consideration that there is a part of you that is making this all up. I want you to understand that we are using your human brain to project the love of the universe through your ego. Your ego gets in the way, like just now with your questioning about all of this. Trust that these messages you are receiving are of a higher element of life than you are currently living.

(When ideas and sentences pop into your head, take into consideration that they aren't coming from you. The angels are communicating with you.)

Wow. I don't even know where to go from here, so I'll just ask if there is anything else you'd like to share today.

Gabriel: That is all there is, Beau. I love you! Till tomorrow! Bye!

Ha! Bye, Gabriel. Bye, Orion.

Hi, Gabriel! Hi, Orion! Gabriel, it's always fun to channel you. Your entrance always brings a smile to my face!

> **Gabriel:** And I know that it does, which is why I do what I do—to make sure you smile. Keep at it, Beau, for *your life is a magical movie of delight and wonder.*

My life is a movie?

> **Gabriel:** This is the next lesson that we can talk about, for yes, your life is a movie and you are not only the director but you are the leading role—and you should win an Oscar for this!

Wow, that's interesting to think about. Not only am I the director of the movie but I'm the leading role. Can you expand on this?

> **Orion:** Picture yourself as the director, but even more than that, as the writer of the script. You are writing not only everything on the spot, but you are directing how people react to you, how they respond to you. If you write yourself as getting upset in a scene, then the outcome and response of others will probably not be to your liking. Keep writing, Beau.
>
> The junction between you and the character you are observing in the guest role is about to be expanded. They react the way you write them in. If you write them in as someone who is hard of hearing (meaning someone who doesn't always hear what you have to say and is therefore fully reactive to your words), then they are going to react in a way you may not like—yet that is how you wrote them in. You are choosing the characters that you write in. For the most part, no person in particular is meant to be written in. You are choosing it.

Now, there are characters that do have to be written in to expand your growth, like a parent or sibling or teacher or boss or best friend. But know that the magical part of all of this is how you write yourself. This is key, Beau. You choose not only how the other characters are written in, but you get to choose how to write your own character in. Isn't it absolute magic?

(For the most part, we get to write in the characters in our own play/life? That makes sense when we unexpectedly bring someone in who can help further our goals and dreams. I also love that we "write" our own part. This is a reminder that we can choose on the spot how to be and how to react to things that happen.)

That *is* magic. We are the scriptwriter, the director, *and* the lead actor. I definitely deserve an award for that!

(Wait ... I am directing, starring, and playing the leading role? I have to put that on my résumé. Next trip: The Academy Awards!)

Orion: And yet, in Hollywood, you don't always see that.

That's crazy. I guess not everything is worth an award. I could write a crappy script and be a horrible actor. Ha! That wouldn't be deserving of an award. What else can you share? Gabriel, would you like to chime back in?

Gabriel: Know that you are on the right path with all of this! Keep going! To further expand on this, know that you are the expression of everything you create. You are writing this script, right? You get to choose what you write! How awesome is that?

(That really is awesome, right? We truly are the creators of our life.)

That sounds identical to what was discussed in the film *The Secret*. You get to write down what you want to appear in your world, visualize it, and then take the actions to make it happen. Is that what you mean, Gabriel?

Gabriel: Uh-huh, yup, yessiree Bob!

You're funny! So are you saying that creating our life is that easy? All we have to do is write it down (scriptwriter), visualize it (director), and then take action on it (lead actor)?

Gabriel: Yes! Also remember that what you write down and how you [expected] to see it is not always what you end up seeing. But know that everything you write down, you will receive. We can also say that when you change your mind or think differently about how a scene will turn out in your head, it changes the script some. That's why it never looks how you envision it.

Remember that people, places, and things get moved around and put in a precise position to make your script/dreams a reality. No movie is ever perfect when the director and company are funding it. Mistakes happen. More importantly, life happens. Know that everything you are doing and creating is your decision and your decision only. No one else is writing your script. No one else is directing your life. Some people think that God does that. God is an audience member who sometimes "interferes" with your "movie" to help things go smoother or to help lead you (as the main character) in the right direction to receive what you want.

Picture God as the company that is funding your movie. Sometimes, that company has more power over you. Remember, though, that God will never do anything to try and defeat you, lead you the wrong way, or completely ruin what you're creating. God helps those who help themselves and sometimes even those who don't.

(I know I have always tried to force an outcome. It's clear after reading this again that that doesn't work. Take charge of your life, but forcing an outcome isn't necessary.

Also, it's my understanding that you must take some kind of action for something you wrote down to show up.)

Are you saying that God is choosy?

Gabriel: No. Not at all. Sometimes people have certain missions or agreements they must fulfill, and if they aren't going in the right direction, then God will come in and move them in the right direction. Move = movie. The *I* is you. You are moving yourself. Hence, a motion picture.

What a fascinating observation. Move. Movie. The *I* in *movie* is me or whoever the person is. That's awesome! I love you two! You know me. I love playing with words. Is there anything else you'd like to share?

Orion: Orion here. That is it for today. Enjoy your day and this lesson. We will have more to share with you tomorrow.

Thank you, Orion and Gabriel! I love you two! **M**oving **O**n **V**isualizing *I* **E**nergetically!

Hi, Gabriel and Orion! How are you two?

> **Orion:** The changes you are about to witness are grander than anything you've ever seen. The separation that the planet seems to think there is will soon be healed. The time is coming for the planet to realize that we are all One. *All One* meaning that we are all made of the same "stuff." There is no difference between me and you and your mom and your neighbor and the person whom you consider your worst enemy. When you pass away, you return home just as everyone else and everything else. There is no separation.

I definitely know this. We are all One for sure. What else can you tell me?

> **Orion:** The mind is the most powerful tool that you have. The mind is what helps you see clearly; it sees your future and makes plans and visualizes and helps you make decisions and everything you can think of, for there is no division between physical and spiritual. Physical sight and spiritual sight are interconnected.

That's a little different from what I expected. I never thought about it like that. The physical and spiritual are connected? I thought they were two different things. I think about the phrase "We are spiritual beings having a physical experience." That makes it sound like they are separated. Then again, as I type that, I'm thinking they aren't separate after all. Please explain further.

> **Gabriel:** Hi! OK, so the physical and spiritual are both separate and connected. A better explanation is to say that the world and space are separate and connected. You and God are separate and

connected. You are here on earth, living your life and experiencing things, and yet there is that silver thread that still attaches you back to God. This is why you're One with God and why everyone and everything is connected. There is no separation. Even though we say that you are kind of separated, the reality is you aren't. You may be further away from God in a physical sense, yet you are still the same.

This is similar to what I mean by "the physical and spiritual are separate and still connected." The love that shines from you is a reflection of God. The physical part of you is actually what is underneath the drapery of the spirit. The soul. People think that your physical body holds the soul. It's the other way around. If you look at aura photos, you see how your aura is around you and not inside you. The love that emanates through your life is your God that surrounds you.

God is love. Love is God. God is the Universe. The Universe is God. Love is the Universe. The Universe is love. It's all the same thing, so why would you think that you are separate from God, and what would make you think your physical body is separate from your spirit? Look at it like this. Think of an oyster, then think of the pearl that's inside it. The pearl is part of the oyster, and it is a separate physical element. They are still connected. It's like a mother and its child. There is no separation. Yes, the physical aspect may be different—and there is still no difference. You're all One. We are all One. You are the Universe in physical form. If God is the Universe, then you are God. God is spirit. You are spirit. Do you see where I am going with this, Beau?

(Is this making sense? We are the same regardless of how we look. If we were different, then we would go to different "heavens" after we pass on, but we don't. Every human, every animal, every insect, every plant, etc., is connected on a spiritual level. We all share the same stuff energetically.)

That was magical! Yes, I do. There may be a separation through our physical sight, but we are all One. We are all connected. It seems like this is one of the lessons, if not *the* main lesson, to get throughout all of these conversations. We are all One. We are all connected. There is *no* separation. Even the acronym for *courage* you gave me yesterday is basically another way of saying that we are all One, and once we realize that, there is nothing to be afraid of.

> **Orion:** I am glad you realize this. You are. We are. Everything within this universe and even outside of this universe is One. Do you get that, Beau? Really. Think about that. You're all One. O.N.E. Only Now Eternally.

That's a really cool acronym, yet I don't know how that expresses that we are all One.

> **Orion:** All there is . . . is Now. Now and Now and Now and Now and Now. If you take the time to consider that if you are God and God is the Universe, and the Universe only operates as Now, then you will realize that the acronym I just gave you makes sense for the message you just received.

(Wow, that's powerful!)

So, if the Universe only operates as Now, and we are the Universe, then *we* operate as Now. Now is all there is. We are all there is, for we are all One. This One that we are only operates in Now. One Now. It seems a bit abstract, but I get it. Interesting.

> **Gabriel:** I am glad you get it. It's really very simple, Beau. One. Now. The only difference in letters is the e in *one* and the w in *Now*. W and e. *We*.

I realized that connection before you typed that! That's amazing, Gabriel. Wow!

(Wow is right! Even reading this over two years later, I find this incredible.)

Gabriel: Amazing, right? I love this. The explosions of emotion you are expressing are so fun to watch, and I love that you are getting it!

I'm done. I don't know what else can be said at this point. Wow.

Orion: The only thing left to say is that we love you more than you can understand as a human being. I love you always and forever and so does Gabriel.

I love you two, as well. Thank you for everything! Bye!

Hi, Gabriel! Hi, Orion! I would like to clear up what we discussed yesterday, not only about being One but also about being the Now. Is that more in the sense that because we are *creating* the Now, it makes *us* the Now? We are creating ourselves moment by moment, and each moment is happening right now. So that would make us the Now. We are the creators of our world. We are the Now. Is that how you mean it?

> **Gabriel:** You are getting it! This is amazing, Beau! I am so proud of you!

Also, you labeled God as Almighty. Since you and Orion have said that there is no "us" and no "them"—there is only "all"—could you say that since we are all One, and if you label God as Almighty, it can be written as All Mighty? We are mighty? Is this a possibility?

> **Gabriel:** You are finally starting to understand the concepts I present to you in the channelings. Be aware that you already know everything there is to know. You just have to be reminded.

(This makes me feel that we were born with a cheat sheet. In other words, the answers are already inside us. We don't have to go looking for truth.)

I believe that. I'm glad I could clear that up. What would you two like to share with me today?

> **Orion:** Orion here. The expression of the being that you are is the concept of God being human. There are certain things that could only be understood in the form of life that you are in. That is also why there are things like birds and caterpillars and all other living beings, like plants. God wanted to know what it was like to be all of these things. The challenge is to really understand and grasp this concept.

You may think, who would want to be a one-legged bird? God would. This is hard to understand, I know. Bear with me. That is also why the universe and everything in it is infinite. There are endless possibilities to life and death. The realm of existence is vast and hard to grasp for you.

You're telling me! After an explanation like that, I'm so lost.

Orion: And there is nothing to get lost in. The only thing that holds you back from believing or understanding a lot of these concepts is fear. Doubt. It has nothing to do with intelligence level. If you believe in this stuff, you should believe in yourself. You are vast and otherworldly. You as a human being are one of the most powerful elements in existence. The things you can do as a human being are limitless. What is stopping any of you from achieving greatness?

Some of you do it. A lot do. Not as many as you would think, though. The vast majority of people live in fear of life. They are afraid of what they're really capable of. A lot of people don't have that fearless mentality. The book of your life is written in your mind, full of lies and defense. Be patient and be aware that your power is extraordinary. Know your power. You can achieve anything!

Thanks for that pat on the back, Orion. That was really nice to hear.

(I'm doing the happy dance.)

Orion: If you only knew your power, Beau. If you understood what you were capable of and stopped living in fear of certain things, you would be a lot further in your life with regard to where you want to be. The only thing stopping your growth is you—and you alone. Remember that you are the only person/thing in control of your life. No one and no thing else. Be aware of this on the rest of your journey. Only you can prevent forest fires.

(I felt Orion gave a cute smile after that little joke.)

Ha! OK, Smokey. I get it, though. I am more powerful than I realize. It is so much easier said than done, though!

> **Orion:** What if I reminded you about courage and the acronym? It basically was another way of saying that we are all One. Once you realize that you are all connected and that everyone is just a reflection of you, you won't be so scared. Then again, as you just realized, you are afraid of yourselves, so it's understandable why some of you would be afraid of someone else. Again, we are all One. If you are afraid of yourself, then it's understandable why you're afraid of others.
>
> Not everyone is. I understand why, though, you're afraid of others. There are people out there who are afraid of themselves and still speak with others and are scared in the process. That is courage. That is what it takes. There is nothing to fear but fear itself. Beau, life on earth is really easy. No one said it was going to be a walk in the park, and yet it's easy. You get in your own way, always. That's it. Obstacles come and go. Struggle comes and goes. Go after your dreams. That is what God put you here for (amongst a large number of other things.) You are here to create. That's it. It's that simple. You are God in human form, and God is a creator. God is the Universe. You are the Universe in human form.

(The message that we are all One is repeated numerous times throughout these channelings. Also, to know that we get in our own way as often as we do is a reminder to us that while we can't stop things from happening, we can choose how to take them. We also can choose whether or not to do something we're afraid to do. This message is so powerful.)

We have a tendency to put so many limits on ourselves. So many concepts you just mentioned have already been shared, and it's nice to be reminded. What is something new you or Gabriel can teach me?

Gabriel: Gabriel here. Remember that One and Now have the letters *w* and *e*, which spells *we*. We are all connected! Yay!

You're like a child, Gabriel. Ha!

Gabriel: We are all God's children. More importantly, what if you lived life with that same imagination and excitement you had as a kid? Use my being as a model!

Be fearless. Live life as a child. Are you saying that you want us to live life as a fearless child?

Gabriel: No. What I want you to be is powerful.

I thought we already *are* powerful, Gabriel.

Gabriel: Keep going.

If we are . . .

Gabriel: Stop right there. You almost gave up. This is what you do. Things get hard and you give up. "Hard" is a decision. You've trained yourself to give up when things get hard, whether it's physically hard or mentally hard or emotionally hard. Don't give up, Beau. Keep working at your growth. Your expansion. The love inside of you is larger than the Universe itself.

You do realize that the glass ceiling you're hitting is fear? The growth that you want to be experiencing is right there for you to grasp, and you're afraid to reach it. You don't think you're that smart, that talented, or that vast in knowledge. What if I told you to stop thinking so much when you channel and just let us type? Believe in our words, for there is only truth that we speak. Orion and I are here as teachers to guide you through life and help make life easier. We are also here to share with you the vastness of the universe. There is another level you can hit if you choose to do so. You can shatter that glass ceiling. You have to trust us.

(I was definitely getting frustrated with the same themes showing up repeatedly. I was ready for a change. I'm reminded of the common phrase "I'm sick and tired of being sick and tired." I was ready for a change in discussion. Let's see where this new road takes me/us.)

I'm ready. I trust you. What else is there to get?

Gabriel: The only thing that stops you is you, so let's get right to it. The majority of you are so afraid of what else is out there, so listen to me clearly. Fear nothing, for everything I am going to share with you is true. The vastness of the universe is complex for the human brain to understand, and that is OK. You don't have to understand everything. There are galaxies that are so transmuted to your identity that the words *universe* and *otherworldly* are a bit foreign to you. Don't worry. I am here to let you know that there is all safety around you.

The channeling that is going on with Beau is ready to hit a new level, so be prepared. The world is coming to an end. By this, I mean the world that you understand and live in. The new world is upon you. It is with you and there is nothing to fear. Be aware that the changes you are seeing currently and will be seeing are only here to further expand the planet. The channelings of Beau are so vast and full of knowledge that you will have to keep up. The stories I will be sharing with you are true and here to teach you more about life. The existence of God is within you. You are part of God. The majority of beings on this planet are not connected to each other like they are capable of. So many of you think that you're separate, but that will soon change. The beings of the planet are here to grow and expand. Be aware that every channeling from here on out will be at a new level of communication.

Wow . . . that was intense. I am excited!

Gabriel: So are we. Yay!

OK, well, I guess we'll get into it tomorrow? Thank you, Gabriel and Orion.

Orion: Beau, you are welcome. We love you.

Gabriel: One more thing, Beau. The energy you receive during channelings will be expanded, and you will notice it on a physical level. It's nothing so major that you should be scared. Just know the level will be raised.

OK. Got it. Thank you! Bye!

Gabriel: Bye, Beau!

Hi, Gabriel! Hi, Orion! We're about to go deeper than usual with these channelings, correct?

Gabriel: Why yes, we are! Are you ready?

Ready as I'll ever be! Let's go!

(I didn't realize how much further we were going to go. This goes quite far down the rabbit hole, in my opinion.)

Gabriel: It's time to delve into a new generation of thought. I want you to consider that everything I'm about to tell you is pure fact, for the universe is grand and there is nothing you can do about that. Listen closely, for the time has come for you to listen to your instinct, Beau. This also goes for everyone else.

The business of the planet is about growth—and only growth. Love is involved as well, for growth is part of loving thyself. Know your intuition is key, and love is the answer to everything. Growth is another word for love. So is instinct. Trust your love. Love is all there is. A lot of people on the planet seem to have forgotten that, and that is OK.

It's time to wake up. The challenge of being human is to be aware that you are all connected, loved, appreciated, and powerful beyond your wildest imagination. Love comes before you in the mirror every day. This goes back to loving thyself. Once you love yourself, the world is your oyster. Remember the metaphor of the pearl still being part of the oyster though it is separated physically? Think of yourself as the pearl since the world is your oyster. You're still the same. You're still connected, and there is nothing to be challenged by in your thoughts. The master being of life is you. You are God. Do you understand this?

(I love the metaphor of us and the Universe being like a pearl and oyster. We are the pearl and the Universe is the oyster. It is separate physically but there is a part of the oyster in the pearl. It sounds like a mother and her child. We are God's/the Universe's children, after all.)

Yes. I do. Since we are all connected, we are God in human form.

> **Gabriel:** Gabriel here. OK, good. So know that the God that you understand is within you and you can achieve anything this God can create and acquire. The world as you know it will not survive how it should if you as a planet don't realize this connection. You're all the same. The pollution of the planet is a reflection of the pollution of you as a people. There are clean parts, and there are much dirtier parts. Cherish the ways of the world, for there is so much to give, so much to experience, and so much to love. All there is, is love. It's just that simple. Now you can consider that you are love. God is love. The Universe is love. Therefore, all you need is yourself. Self-love. Love thyself. It really is simple, Beau.

Wow.

> **Gabriel:** I know! The planet is you. You are the pearl of the oyster, and all the connectivity is the same. The being that you are controls the fate of the world. You all are in control. There is no hiding from this. Cherish your love. Love, love, love, love. The world is into changing itself to better itself, and love is all there is. The being that you are is here to extrapolate the functions within you and help better each other. The world is all there is. The Universe is all there is. You are all there is. You're all the same. We are all the same. Be with that.

(That is an incredibly strong message: "We are all the same." In other words, we are all One.)

If I am responsible for myself, and I am one with the planet, then I am responsible for the planet?

Gabriel: Yes, you are. Know that you are responsible for your whole, entire life, from beginning to end. The world needs to breathe. The world needs to realize how powerful it is. You see, the world does what it has to do to survive and grow. What if you lived like that? You know what you have to do, but you're afraid at times to grow and do those things. I love you, Beau. Love is you. Therefore, you are the matter of essential being for the planet. Every ounce of you is the key element to the level of acceptance there is to mature on the planet. The being that controls the fate of your world (inside and out) is you and you alone.

(We control our whole life. That's why I feel the message of taking 100 percent responsibility is repeated so often. It is so important to control our life at every moment possible to achieve the future we want.)

That's really fascinating. I'm really intrigued and amazed at how we are not only the planet and the universe, but we are fully responsible for the planet and universe. I can understand how we as a people are responsible for the planet, but how are we responsible for the universe, especially if it's infinite?

Gabriel: And so now is the time to expand on this. God is in control and the creator of the universe, correct?

Yes.

Gabriel: OK, good. So remind yourself that you are God in human form.

OK. I am God in human form.

Gabriel: You are taking the idea [that] you are in charge of the universe too seriously, and more importantly, too literally. The way you take care of yourself is how the planet looks. How the planet is resting in the universe is how the universe is being taken care of on your end. Know that you are adding too much complexity to this equation. Be you. Take care of yourself and the planet will follow suit. Know that the majority of your life is taking care of yourself. The planet is a reflection of you. Know that the world is your oyster. Therefore, you are the planet and the planet is you, and that means the universe is you. Take care of yourself, which will take care of the planet, which will take care of the universe. Give the universe something to be comfortable with.

Take care of myself and the planet will take care of itself, and therefore, the universe will take care of itself. It's like a chain reaction.

Orion: There is the next lesson: *Not only are you the same, but you're all linked together with a universal energy chain.*

Please discuss this chain in more detail.

Gabriel: The chain is the quintessential element amongst all of you and all of us. There is no need to establish a master or anything like that, for the universe is here to be one with the planet and one with you. Since you are God, there is no "master." Do you understand this?

I think so. Does that mean we *are all* God? We *are all* in control? We *are all* creators? You're saying the Universe is a creator?

Gabriel: The Universe created the earth, didn't it?

I thought God did that. Then again, if God is another word for the Universe, then yes, God/the Universe *did* create the planet. Wouldn't that mean, though, that *we* (human beings) created the planet? Does that mean the planet created itself?

Gabriel: If you look at it in the way that you're all One, then yes.

(Mind is officially blown.)

So we can say that we as One grew with the creation of the universe and then the creation of the Earth and all other stars and planets?

Orion: Yes, this is correct. You're all One. You created everything. Also remember that everything around you is just your thoughts.

This can be understood in so many ways. It's my understanding that we create everything in the mind first and then bring it to physical reality. That's a thought. The Universe in its "thought"—or whatever you would call it at that level—thought about creating a universe and then did it. This can also be discussed as what I've read and heard, that life is just perception and that everything doesn't necessarily exist. If I'm told a tree is in front of my window, then there is a tree in front of my window. Even if I weren't told that, but many people were aware of it, then it would exist. This is why blind people are living in this world how they are. Even though they can't *see* something, others know it exists. Therefore, it is here in physical reality. This whole concept is nuts.

Orion: You are on the right track, Beau. You are creating your reality. Be responsible for it—100 percent responsibility is key for having the life you want.

(There's the 100 percent responsibility statement again. If it's repeated this often, then it is a very important message that is coming through.)

This whole channeling has been a lot to take in, and with that, I must end this and let this all soak in. Thank you so much, Gabriel and Orion.

Orion: You are welcome, Beau.

Gabriel: Bye, Beau!

Hi, Gabriel! Hi, Orion. I look forward to this morning's channeling! What can you share?

Orion: Know that your soul is part of God and that everything you do is a discussion for God. By that, I mean that God is experiencing life through you. The vast majority of the planet doesn't understand this concept, but it is changing. There is no fear for you to have. Everything is working out perfectly.

Gabriel: Ready? Here we go. The ego is a self-defense mechanism to keep you small. The ego is good because it keeps you safe and out of harm's way at times, and you also have the free will to do what you want. The discussion of God living through you is related to the ego. The triumph of cooperation between you and God happens when the ego is not in control. The moment that ego takes over is when your humanness kicks in. There is nothing wrong with that. It is part of being human. Know your greatest adversary is yourself. There is no being on the planet or off the planet that reigns supreme in your life except you—and only you. The chief command for you to understand is that there is no Spirit without Being. The spirit is being.

The spirit is being? What do you mean by that? Please better explain this in simple terms, Gabriel.

Gabriel: Absolutely. The spirit is being in the sense that you are a human being. Also, it means that the calculated substance that is you is the spirit, and the spirit doesn't exist as just a spirit. The spirit *is*. Do you understand this? There is no you without spirit. There is no spirit without God. You are a human being, so why wouldn't there be a spirit being?

This is a bit abstract. I'm having trouble understanding this. Please explain more.

Orion: The spirit is everything. Everything is Being. The planet is Being. You are Being. God is Being. What if I put "a" in front of that? You are a being. God is a being. The Universe and the Earth are beings, so the spirit is a being. Remember, this goes back to the discussion of *Now*. You are Now. The Universe is Now. Therefore, *Now* is another word for Being. Now is Being. You are Now. You are Being. The Universe is Now. The Universe is Being. The spirit is Now, so the spirit is Being. All there is, is Now. All there is, then, is Being.

(You are Now because Now is all there is. Life is truly better when you're in the moment. When you're in the moment, you are Now. Now backwards is Won. *When you are in the Now, you've won!)*

OK. It's out there, but I think I get it. Everything is happening now, for Now is all there is. With that said, everything is Being because Being is all there is. We can't be any other way. That's an interesting concept, Orion.

Orion: You know what's even cooler than that? You are a being, being.

Ha! I like that! OK, I get it now. What else would you two like to share?

Gabriel: Now we can get into the conversation about the exit strategy from being closed-minded to being open-minded. The beings that you are, are closed off, for the most part. I say that because not all of you are, but enough of you still think that you're separate from each other. This world, this life, is not about you. It's about something much greater. Even greater than God, and that is the essence of these conversations.

I believe that. All of these discussions have a foundation of "We are all One." Please share more.

Orion: The planet is coming to an end, and that was discussed in a past conversation. The earlier you realize as a planet that you're all the same is a way to bring this new world quicker and closer. The essence of life lies in how you treat each other. Wars, fights, separation . . . it all keeps you away from each other. Know that your role on this planet is to recognize that you're all One. You're all the same. Please understand this. There is no thing and no one to be afraid of. Keep your mind open to the possibility that you're all connected. The world and life in general is not coming to an end unless you keep fighting and end life yourselves. Even then, it will live on. Be aware that your world and the fate of it is up to you. Be love.

(Remember, the physical world that we live on is not ending. There is a big change happening on the planet. We as a human race are evolving.)

There's nothing else to say about that, is there?

Gabriel: Nope.

Is there anything else you'd like to share with me?

Take that in for today! We love you!

I love you, too. Bye!

Hey, Gabriel and Orion! What would you like to share with me in this channeling?

Orion: Know the time has come to reveal a new secret to you. This is the secret that stops so many people from achieving their goals. There is [so much] doubt in so many people's hearts that it can be tough to maneuver through. Everything happens for a reason, and your goal is not to make it mean anything and to continue to plow through whatever you're dealing with.

You are God in human form. God doesn't get stopped. Any issues that are happening, God deals with. There is always a way around everything. It wouldn't be placed in your way without another way to go around it. It's really that simple. So many human beings give up when things get too hard. Know that the time has come for you to know that there's no such thing as fear. Fear is made up. The saying goes that there is nothing to fear but fear itself. Remember that fear is not a physical element. Fear is not a wall. Fear is nothing. Therefore, there is nothing to fear. Literally. Fear doesn't exist in physical reality.

(That's so great to be reminded of, all these years later. Fear doesn't exist in physical reality. It's not a thing with four legs and teeth that chases you, nor is it a bug or virus. Therefore, it doesn't exist. Think about that.)

Wow. That was powerful. I never thought of it like that. Thanks for sharing that. What else can you share with me?

Gabriel: Gabriel is present now! The time has come to reveal that there is no goal that *has* to be met. Life is a choice. Life is a journey. Now, you do have certain promises, or rather new ways of handling certain situations that you said you would do before you came to earth. Yet, if *you* don't do them, then someone else will. Where there is a will, there is a way. You don't have to believe anything I'm telling you. Know it is true. The documented life that you currently live is being channeled through you by God. A reminder that God lives through you, for God experiences life through you. Everyone is part of that journey. Be gracious and don't forget that.

So are you saying that we live for God? That sounds like something out of the Bible.

Gabriel: Nope, not at all. You live for *you*. God only experiences.

But if something has to get done, then God will assist to get it done, correct?

Gabriel: That is correct! That doesn't mean that you live for God—you live for *you*. Then again, you are God in human form and you're all One, so technically, yes, you do live for God, if you look at it that way.

So why were humans made? Isn't all of this something that God could have experienced Itself?

Gabriel: You think it's that simple.

It's not?

Orion: The only thing that is simple is the way you understand it as a human being. Your intelligence can only stretch so far. This doesn't mean that humans are dumb. *Far* from it. You're all geniuses. That said, the human brain can't understand everything when it comes to space, God, and all that. It is impossible. Some people will read this and fight it and might even feel insulted.

Again, humans are geniuses. Know that you are a genius, Beau. There is no fault in your intelligence. Remember that God's/the Universe's intelligence is infinite. It had to create infinity. It created infinite galaxies and stars and everything else you can imagine. It created you, animals, and plants perfectly. Down to a T. There are no mistakes in the Universe, for it doesn't make mistakes. Know that there is an intelligence that is even stronger than yours. That doesn't mean that you're stupid at all.

(I know we're not stupid, but that was a lot to take in. I don't know about you, but I need a moment!)

That's a hard concept to grasp.

Orion: And so it is.

What else would you like to share?

Gabriel: Gabriel here! The galaxies are contemplating a universal shift within the plateau of universes. The astral planes are melding together to form one big galaxy. The space/time continuum is infinite and will expand even farther than it already has. The time has come for a shift. The universe is growing. Isn't that hard to imagine when the universe is infinite? How do you expand infinity?

Easy. You say it will, and you do it. You see, that's what's funny about humans. You think that you can only go so far. All you have to do is write it down and execute it. Things will work out in your favor, and they don't always look how you expect. Know that you are the creators of your world, and it's as simple as that. I love you, Beau!

I love you too, Gabriel. I don't even know what else to ask you and Orion during this channeling. If there is anything either of you would like to share, please do so.

Orion: The universe is based on three things: 1) love, 2) faith, and 3) faith. There is a difference in those two faiths. One is a faith of believing everything will work out, and the other is a faith that everything will be OK. Those sound similar, but they are different. Let me explain further.

(If this isn't making any sense, keep reading. It will.)

The world that you understand is growing and expanding, and so for that growth to happen, it must be taken charge of by the universe. The human race as a whole can only reach a certain point until something larger has to take the lead. This doesn't mean that you are dumb. Again, I mentioned that you can do *anything*. This also means that you can do anything and then it still has to be polished up, and things have to be done that you as human beings don't understand. The life you live is under reconstruction, and the knowing of the Universe will take over and complete its mission.

Gabriel: Yay! OK, so the Universe will take over where you can no longer expand, and that's fine. The Universe is taking over from there. The Universe will expand itself to even larger infinite levels. God is the Universe. The Universe is God. God is expanding. You are God in human form. Humans are expanding. Think of the 2012 shift you're going through. You're expanding. You're reaching a new way of life. It may not look it right now in some parts of the world, but know you are expanding. And this is where we will end today's session. I love you!

Ha! OK. I love you, too. Bye!

Hi, Gabriel and Orion! I apologize about not channeling first thing when I woke up, like I've been doing.

> **Gabriel:** Beau, there is no concern for that. The word is for you to understand that as long as you are still doing it today, then you are fine. Even if you missed a day, it's OK. Your life is *your* creation. If you can't do this, then someone else will.

I just want to make sure *I'm* the one creating my life. You gave me this gift, and I plan on using it to its fullest extent.

> **Orion:** This is a great attitude, for much success will come from these channelings for you. Success will also come to the world. Be aware that everything you are writing is going to impact people so positively, in ways that you can't imagine right now. It's OK. I love you.

I love you too, Orion. So do you want to pick up where we left off yesterday, or is there new information you'd like to give me?

> **Gabriel:** The time has come to go even further with these channels. Let me take the wheel for a minute . . . . The world has come to a point of transcending, and now is the time to expand on the growth that you call life. Life is expanding rapidly, and the only way to make all of this work for you is to be cooperative. You don't have a choice, for the Universe and planet Earth will do what they have to do. You can only follow suit, and that is fine, for everything will work out according to plan.

(In other words, the Earth will take care of itself. There is no need to worry about it.)

There's a plan? That almost makes it sound like God doesn't care about us, just the planet. Am I wrong?

Orion: You are very wrong about that. God knows what is best for the universe, for the world, and especially for you as a human race. Don't be disturbed or worried, for there is a reason for everything. Know that you are here for a mission larger than you realize, and that is OK.

There is no secret for you to understand. You are here to live, know, and experience everything. The thing is, even if we told you what was happening, you might not believe it because it might sound so far-fetched and so out of this world that it would be hard to believe. It also might be hard for you to grasp, and that's OK too. Love is all there is, Beau. Remember this and know that everything is done from a place of love. It is a love that you do not understand. It is different from the love that humans understand. It is grander. It is exquisite. It is cherishing. You are love in human form. Know that everything you are being told is the truth.

That was beautiful, Orion! Wow. You've shared that with me more times than I can remember—that we're made of love. Why are you sharing this with me again?

Orion: It is because there are still people out there that will read this who might not believe that you as people are made of love. Love is love is love is love is love.

That's awesome. What else can you share with me?

Gabriel: The universe is changing shape. You as a soul are changing shape. The universe is growing and expanding and shifting, and know that everything that it is going through, you are also going through. You, Beau, are changing. Everyone and everything on the planet is changing physically and energetically to be prepared for the New World.

Please share with me more about this New World. What does it look like?

Gabriel: The New World is everything you dreamt of and never even realized you wanted. So many people on the planet want their dreams to come true. They want their dreams a reality. Their thoughts are a reality. Everything. Well, that's what you're getting. The world has been through a lot over the past few hundred years, and the people deserve what is coming. The planet is a teacher, and you are the students. You went through your course as a society, you passed with flying colors, and now you are being rewarded. Yay!

(We passed? Thank goodness! Look at me now, Ma!)

What is this reward you speak of?

Gabriel: As mentioned just before, dreams become reality. Thoughts become reality, but the difference between then and now is that they happen instantaneously. The challenge for you is to get that whatever you think happens immediately in physical reality. The challenge is to learn to control your thoughts. The light energy that maneuvers around you is a giant bird of prey. You are the worms and you are available to be swallowed whole. This sounds bad but it's not.

So please explain that better so it sounds good.

Orion: The bird of prey, which is the light energy, surrounds you and everyone else, and it surrounds the planet. If it "swallows" you (meant metaphorically), then you are part of the light energy. Once you realize this, you can take more control of your life.

(When Archangel Gabriel says thoughts will start to happen instantaneously, take into consideration that angels don't live in linear time like humans do. It may be instant to them, but things may not appear right

away for us. It is my understanding they will happen quickly, though. It also sounds as if how quickly things appear depends on our belief.)

That does sound pretty sweet. Gabriel and Orion, this dinner I just ate knocked me out. I'm ready to go to bed. Is there anything else you'd like to share before I end this channeling session?

> **Gabriel:** No, for the time has come during this session for it to end. We love you.

I love you, too. Bye!

Hello, Orion and Gabriel! What would you like to share with me today?

Gabriel: The human body is made of four centralized, artful, century-old diamonds.

Um . . . what?

Gabriel: Consider that everything I tell you has a deeper meaning and that I also speak to you in metaphors. Consider this.

OK. I am considering that. What do you mean though by "four centralized, artful, century-old diamonds?"

Orion: Take into account that you are made of these same things, being that you have a human body. This is another way of discussing not only your auras but things much deeper than that that are not much talked about within spirituality. This is an old way of communication that was started by a tribe in Africa—Zimbabwe, mostly. The artful, century-old diamond is a response to how they handled the death of a person. Once the body was mummified, they made the decision that the heart was the diamond and that the four valves within the heart were the four diamonds. *Century-old* referred to how long they lived before and after life, as well as the life they lived, for they did not live long on earth due to disease.

I don't even know how to approach this conversation. This is one of those *very* out-there conversations that make me question my ability to channel, so please explain this further.

Orion: The discovery made by this tribe was made by the one who led the tribe. After his queen died young, they discovered this while mummifying her. The cherubs that took over the direction of the soul once the physical life ended were the ones who led them to this discovery. They were also human, so this is how they managed to mourn the loss of their great queen.

(Regarding Orion saying that the cherubs were human, I do fully believe that angels often take the form of a human being. Thus, cherubs appearing as human makes sense to me.)

Please tell me more.

> **Gabriel:** The discovery of these ancient traditions is not known by many, and you will have to do some serious research on this. It exists, and only time will tell. There are some who know, but most do not.

I almost want to finish this channel just to do research on this. Before I do that, what does this have to do with anything else you've taught me?

> **Gabriel:** Consider that I want you to believe what I tell you, regardless of how far-fetched it sounds. There is truth in everything that I tell you. The words given to you are from a higher plane of existence. You are not making this up. Know the truth is within you, and just like anything else, some things take hard work to figure out. Do your research on this and you will see the connection.
>
> Also, don't take anything at face value. This may not look identical to what you find, but there are stories out there about this that strongly resemble it. Know I speak only truth to you.

OK. I'll believe you. I want to go and do research on this right now, though.

(I researched this for more clarity, but I couldn't find anything. Let me know if you do.)

Is there anything else you'd like to share before I end this channeling session?

Gabriel: You are God. Be aware of your power.

I will. Thank you for the reminder.

Orion: The journey begins now.

Ha. It does! Bye!

Gabriel, it is always a pleasure to speak with you.

Gabriel: Orion will always be around you, but he will only be on a few more channelings with me. We will soon go back to just me again.

(*I don't know about you, but I'm sad about that. Orion has been fun to channel. I loved Orion's energy, too. It's so relaxing. Orion is also unfathomably wise. I'm guessing you're also constantly blown away by what Orion shares. Hopefully, it's not just me!*)

What is something new you'd like to share with me?

Gabriel: The time has come for you to let go of the wheel and just let me talk. The words and ideas that are perpetuating from your skull are the exact wise ways for the Universe, and how I communicate with you is not as important as the message being sent. Don't think anything happening is fake, for you are channeling a higher energy than you. It is like your mom and even Halley have said. You are channeling a different voice. A distinct voice. I come across to you differently than I come across to others. That's just how you channel my energy. The messages are always the same though.

(*A reminder that Halley is the empowerment psychic who wrote the foreword to my first book of channels with Archangel Gabriel, called* Gabriel's Guidance.)

So please go ahead and share what you have to share. Use me as your channel during this process.

Gabriel: I am doing that. Let's begin with the fact that you are in fact made of star stuff. The world is the Universe is you is God is Nature. I will repeat this message throughout these channelings to get the point across. The words and ideas expressed within these channelings are universal truths that some will get and some won't. What needs to happen is that there needs to be a tilt, a shift within the thinking of the human brain amongst enough people. The words that come to you are for the world—not just you and your mom. Why do I say this? Because it is easy to get caught up in the self-growth amongst yourselves. Use these words and let other people know about the magic gateway to a whole other universe full of love and wonder.

(I was living back at home at the time of the channels, and I showed my mom all of them. I am putting these books out for the world to read. I believe it is so important to share these messages with all of you.)

I am so tempted to share each channeling with the world as it comes in, and I have to stop myself. Aside from these messages for the world, I feel like these are also here to help me financially, and keep me secure. Am I wrong? Am I being greedy?

Gabriel: Absolutely not. The *Conversations with God* books made Neale Donald Walsch rich. Why wouldn't these books support you the same way? Spirit will always support you.

OK. Enough about me. What else would you like to share with me and the rest of the world?

Gabriel: Absolutely do whatever you want with your life. Stop thinking about the consequences of your actions. Be smart in your ways and don't do anything that is going to hurt or harm another human being or *any* other living creature, whether an animal or something from Nature like a plant or tree or even the earth, like its water. Its water is the blood of the earth.

Gabriel, are you saying we're vampires?

> **Gabriel:** No, silly. What I am saying is that you are drinking the life blood of the earth. Remember, you're all the same. You're living off your own energy. Same goes with plants and animals. You're living off your own energy.

(This is confirmation for me that we should treat each other with kindness and love.)

That's a fascinating concept. I never looked at it like that. What else can you share?

> **Gabriel:** The world is one living, breathing organism. You are part of that, for you are on the earth. Take into consideration that you are like the cells of the planet and the planet and galaxies are like the cells of the universe. Also, consider that the universe is like the heart of God. Then again, Beau, remember that God is the Universe.

I'm getting confused now. If everything is everything, and God is the Universe, which is also us, then how does what you said make sense regarding us being the cells of the planet and the planets being cells of the Universe, etc.? I don't even know what to think or believe.

> **Gabriel:** The conceptual outlook that you have will never truly be readable to the human mind, for the human mind can truly only expand so far. I can tell you so many things that would continue to [challenge] your beliefs and [make you] question whether or not any of this is real.

(I'm already there!)

Why don't you come through as strong as I sometimes expect you to come through? It's a big part of why I feel like I'm making this up. I feel like my identity is making all of this up. It's doing what it has to do to stay alive.

Gabriel: Don't ever question any of this.

Well, I am. Ha!

(I am such a goofball.)

Gabriel: There is no need to do that, for I can tell you things that will make you realize that this is not fake. How far would you like to go down the wormhole, Beau?

Let's go deep.

Gabriel: The energetic field that surrounds you is called an immaculate breed of ancestors' words that are labeled as human. It is where the word *human* came from, and know that all of this is true. The words and ideas that are expressed were known by native cultures, and the words and ideas shared with you were (to an extent) understood by past tribes and other cultures. The current planet in certain areas is so covered by the cloak of darkness that you currently possess, with some of you poking holes in it to see the light. The light will always shine through in the dark. Light penetrates dark always. That is why there is more positivity than negativity. It may not look like it, but there is.

(I heard once that the word human *means "hue man." We are all different shades. Man, this is getting deep.)*

Let's go further down the wormhole, Gabriel, starting now.

Gabriel: The intergalactic time portal that helps you see your past and future is linked to your brain, and more so, your mind is the essence of who you are, and it is why you are able to create your life through thought.

(This is nuts! Archangel Gabriel isn't saying anything new, but it's profound. We create our life through thought. Our past and future only exist in our mind. Our past is created by our memories, and our future is created

through imagination or daydreams. As I said, this isn't really anything new regarding what Gabriel has said, but it's worded in such a profound way.)

That definitely makes sense. Let's go even further down the wormhole. What else can you tell me?

> **Gabriel:** The truth of the Universe is within you. Why do you think that when you type a lot of this information I share with you, you feel like you already know it? It happened often with the life lessons. None of this is new to you. The truth is within you. *Always* look inside. The truth is there. It always has been and always will be.

So am I right to consider that, if we are made of the Universe, then the truth is the Universe itself?

> **Gabriel:** You got it. Keep going. What else do you realize?

If we are God in human form, then God is the truth? I realize that sounds a little religious, but it's not meant that way. God is the Universe. God is us. We are God. We are the Universe, so the truth truly is within us.

> **Gabriel:** Good. I am glad you are beginning to understand this.

(A reminder that we are God/the Universe in human form.)

Let us go even deeper in the wormhole. What else can you share?

> **Gabriel:** We can go back to what I shared with you in a life lesson: If you are God in human form and also the Universe, then this is you typing.

While I completely understand that *so* much differently now, that still makes me question a lot of this. It's moments like this I sit here looking out my window wondering if I'm crazy. I am also realizing that I am connected to the trees and grass outside my window, as well as all of the stuff on my desk, like my computer mouse, my cell phone, and my water bottle (and the water in it!). As I look around at what's on my desk and realize I'm connected to everything, I now fully understand the idea of aligning my energy with what I want to see come into my life. This is awesome to realize!

(I hope that's as eye-opening to you as it was for me. We are all One.)

> **Gabriel:** So the time has come to tell you that you are completely wrong.

What?

> **Gabriel:** The energy of the things you want has to align with you. You are a spiritual being having a physical experience. You want the energy of other things to align with *you*. Be who you want to become. Watch those things start to show up.

(That can be confusing, considering I just said we're all One. What I feel Gabriel meant by this is that whatever we want to bring into our life must match our energy. If I want to be a music star, then I have to bring that energy into my life. It's a matter of thinking about it, feeling it in my heart, and then taking action, while letting the Universe do the rest.)

Wow, Gabriel. That's a really interesting way of looking at it. I never even considered that. Thank you.

> **Gabriel:** You're welcome.

> Is there anything else you'd like to share with me during today's channeling?

> **Gabriel:** Go out into the world today and be who you want to become.

> I will! Bye, Gabriel.

> **Gabriel:** Bye, Beau.

Hey, Gabriel! Hi, Orion! I was glad to see Orion come through, considering that you said he's only going to be around for a few more channeling sessions.

Gabriel: I know! How fun! The fact is that he is here to share the most outrageous and prestigious worldly and otherworldly experiences and truths with you. Here is Orion!

Orion: Know that the time has come for you to go further into your knowledge. The seemingly adverse effects of truth are here to help you stay humble and mature. The truth that sets you apart from others is here for you to realize your greatest potential. The side of your awesome spirit is the side that hides out in your personality. Your true self doesn't want to come out. A lot of humans are not authentically themselves. Be yourself. Be outrageous. Be artistic. Be spectacular. Be extraordinary. Be precious. Be pervasive. Be anything your heart and soul desires, for there is only a limited time on earth that you have to be these things. The amalgamation of force that lies within you is inspiring to the world. Be that.

That was beautiful, Orion. What else can you tell me?

Orion: Know that the charted path for your life is drawn out in your mind. You can draw and write it out on a piece of paper or your computer to make it real and more exquisite, and this is highly recommended by a lot of teachers of this knowledge. Regardless, keep it in your mind who you want to be and where you want to go and what you want to see happen in your life. The choice is yours, and there is nobody else creating your life but you. The majestic syncopation of life beats at a rate that a human being doesn't understand. It is one hundred times the speed of light. Characteristics can flaw you. Choose wisely who you are.

Why am I constantly told the same things over and over, just in different words?

Gabriel: There is only one truth, Beau, and it's the same one talked about over and over again. Thoughts become things. We are all One. Therefore, the thoughts of the Universe created human beings and human beings create their life. Humans are God in human form. The Universe is God. It's really that simple. This is a very easy concept to understand.

Let's go deeper, though, because what's the point of channeling if I'm being told the same thing over and over again? What's something new you can tell me?

Gabriel: Are you ready?

I imagine I am, if I'm asking for more information.

Gabriel: Remember that the sun, moon, and stars are aligned always, even if they don't look like that with your eyes. There is a connection to everything, for everything is a mirror of everything else, just like you are a mirror of everybody and everybody is a mirror of you. Beau, there is *no* separation. I don't know if you're fully getting that yet. The stars, planets, animals, bugs, wildlife in general, Nature, and all its plants and trees and fruits and vegetables . . . if you studied all of these things and studied the human body, you would see that it's all the same thing. Not only are we all made of star stuff, but we're literally built the same way. Cells, brains, hearts, souls, spirit. Some things may be on a different path than others (think about how a plant is on a different kind of life path from a dog), but consider that, deep inside, we're all the same. It's just that simple.

(Holy smokes! This goes really deep. It's more proof that everything on this planet and off this planet is connected, even if just a tiny bit. That is incredible.)

I knew that, but I really never thought about it that deeply. What else can you two share?

Orion: One more thing. Just like God created you, you are creating God.

If God is everything and God is *us,* then yeah, I guess that makes sense. We are creating ourselves and creating how everything shows up to us. God is also experiencing life *through* us. That makes sense.

Orion: OK, good! Yay!

OK, bye!

Orion: Bye, Beau.

Hi, everyone!

Orion: It's great to be with you, Beau. This composition of light between us is coming to a close, and you will be working strictly with Gabriel again. Let me explain more about life and the universe for you. The possibilities are endless. The journey through this dimension begins with one step. One walk. One pioneering, outrageous walk of wisdom, understanding, and valor. There is only so much that can be said about the way a human being can understand this. The universe is so vast that it's endless. Your brain can't possibly understand *endless*. Be aware that the wisdom within you can. This wisdom is your soul, which is your spirit, which is the Universe itself, which is also called God.

The journey therefore begins inside. The walk you must take is a walk inside your mind. Don't be afraid of this. The truth is within you, as we've discussed. Be scared only of the amazing light that will shine upon you. There is nothing to fear, but if you were to fear anything, fear the light that emanates from you and your own power. Don't even be afraid of that. Your strength lies here. Watch, observe, and listen to people who have been able to open up this bottle and release their strength. The silence that spills out is deafening. Only you can take this step within yourself.

(This is where the famous phrase "The only thing we have to fear is fear itself" comes into play. A lot of us are afraid of our own power. In hindsight, I don't know why I ever was.)

That was something else. That was very deep. Where do we go from here?

Orion: The galaxy is endless. So are you. You see, Beau, there isn't much to tell you when we are all connected. Be yourself. Don't fear anything. There is nothing to fear but fear itself. I wouldn't even be afraid of fear. Embrace it and then move past it. The secret to life (if you even want to call it that since there really isn't one) is to be courageous. Courageous in everything you do. Maya Angelou pointed this out. Don't embrace your fears and then think you're safe. You aren't safe. You're trapped in the same loop. Loops repeat. That's why it's called a *loop*. Loop. Pool. You are a drop in the pool. The ocean. Don't look backwards.

You and Gabriel, with your metaphors and acronyms. Outstanding.

Orion: I want you to get, Beau, that whenever you read channelings from other angels, like the channeling of Archangel Raphael you recently read, it was the same idea. Be powerful. Love yourself. Don't go and break the law, but be willing to risk it all for a greater life. Only you can prevent forest fires.

I love that you use that saying to get your point across. I understand it. You're saying it's up to us and only us. If we are going through tough times, it is up to us to clean it up.

Orion: I am happy you understand this. Be One with God. You are God. Be One with yourself.

Understandable. Is there anything else you'd like to share?

Orion: There is nothing else. Here is Gabriel.

Gabriel: Hi, Beau. This expert advice of Orion is something that you should hold on to deeply and never let go. The words of advice you were just given are to be taken into your world and put into everyday use. There is no sequential order for them. Just take them and use them. That is it for today's channeling. Everything is One. I am you. You are God.

Good morning, Gabriel.

> **Gabriel:** Beau, it is always a pleasure communicating with you. I love you. I love that you do this first thing in the morning. This should be a regular routine after we finish these two weeks. Be present to your sophistication and growth over this past week. This is great. Cherish your moments with everyone around you. Life is about Grace and Love. Be kind to others. Love thy neighbor and realize that everyone *is* your neighbor. You all share the same living space. Some of you are just farther away from each other than others.

The planet Earth is massive, and yet you're saying that people in Egypt and China are my neighbors even though China is on the other side of the world from me?

> **Gabriel:** What else would I point to? Besides, you're all the same. You're beside yourself! This doesn't mean anything bad, of course. I say that in humor.

You are quite a character. What new information can you share with me today, Gabriel?

> **Gabriel:** Here it is. Stop procrastinating. I speak to the human race, not just you, Beau. The earth is coming to an end in the way you know it, and it is shifting into a new realm of love and respectful insight. The cherished souls on the journey to a new dawn are here to arrive at the latest and greatest love there has ever been. The walking dead are coming to life, and it is only a matter of time until all of you realize that there is more to life than sex and booze.

So many of you think you're these rock 'n' roll superstars living without a care in the world. You act as if there are no penalties for your actions. I see this happening more in certain areas of the world than others, but all over the world, this happens. Be awake. It is time to come home and acknowledge the fact that you are all from a place much larger and more pristine than you may currently realize. The exquisite insight that has brought you here wants you to know that you are loved. It wants you to know that there is no need to wear a mask of despair every day. There is nothing to hide from. Be yourself. Be the best you. Be great. Be astonishing. Be breathtaking. All there is for you to get is that time heals all wounds. The time has come for you to open your heart and breathe in a sigh of relief. The ones who are open are the ones who will receive these gifts the fastest. The love that pours in from the other side is immense.

(Do you see all the love that is coming to us on this planet? If it doesn't look that way right now—and it may not because we are going through a major shift—I see it, and it is just what we as people need to grow.)

I will say this again. It seems like it's the same message over and over again. What's something new that you can share with me? Something we haven't talked about yet. How about you start sharing new life lessons with me?

Gabriel: The exquisite past of your life is counting on you not to do the same things you once did.

In other words, don't make the same mistakes over and over. Also, it sounds to me like another way of saying "Learn from your past and grow. Keep growing." Am I correct?

Gabriel: You are getting it. Great. Here is another lesson: *Symphonies are only in the mind, and creation is only in the present reality.*

(That's so poetic. Gabriel is saying that we are given ideas by the Universe through thought, and then we create them in the present moment through action. That's beautiful!)

You have such a way with words, Gabriel.

Gabriel: You are me, Beau. *You* have a way with words. *You* are a lyricist.

That I am. What is another new life lesson you can share with me?

Gabriel: I will give you one more channeling before we end this for today: *Love life always and forever, even when times are tough.*

This is much easier said than done.

Gabriel: Right. Only you are the one in charge of your life. Love is a choice. Life is a choice. How you respond to it is a choice.

I felt like I was writing that, not you.

Gabriel: We're all One, Beau.

Yes, we are. OK. I guess that's it, then. Till tomorrow. Bye, Gabriel.

Hello, Gabriel. What would like to share with me this morning?

Gabriel: All of the circumstances that have diminished your confidence are the result of choices made by your subconscious. Awareness of self is important so that you never listen to your ego when it wants to bring you down. The facets of the mind are impervious to joy. Love yourself. Love your reflection. Love everyone and know that the time will come, if you choose for it to come, when you can make the choice to be powerful. Remember that life is a choice and only a choice. Things happen that you cannot control. It is up to you as to how you choose to enhance your being.

Life is a choice. Don't let our ego control us. I understand.

Gabriel: The key to life is to remember that you are in control. This means *100 percent responsibility*. Be responsible for *everything* that happens to you. You create. You react. You bring in who and what your mind thinks about. Only *you* control your mind, so *you* are the one in charge of what it thinks. It's just that simple, Beau. Smile and remember that you are 100 percent responsible for your choices. Life is a journey. You draw the map.

(I didn't realize how important being 100 percent responsible for everything really was. This makes me look at my life in a whole new perspective. Try taking that on yourself. I'd love to hear how being 100 percent responsible for everything has changed your life!)

We are also writing the story, correct?

Gabriel: All of life is the atlas to heaven.

Do you mean that literally or metaphorically?

Gabriel: I mean that both spiritually and physically, as well as mentally.

Easy enough. Can we talk about food and what is the healthiest way for humans to eat? Maybe what key foods we should eat and key foods we should avoid?

Gabriel: I'll make this really simple. Listen to your body and notice how it responds to certain foods. Your body will *always* let you know. The clues are out there if you want to research; there is only so much I can tell you. The truth is that it is different for everybody. Listen to your body. You are also at a point in your civilization that you know what foods are good and bad for you because the information is out there on television, books, and the Internet. You just have to trust your gut (literally).

(It looks like Archangel Gabriel is also a wordsmith.)

Thank you for making that very clear. I guess that goes back to being 100 percent responsible. We must *choose* to do the research and to listen to our body.

Gabriel: Choices. Responsibility. Beau, it is all there for you to appreciate.

OK, so what other new information would you like to share with me? Would you like to share a new life lesson with me?

Gabriel: The love that expands from your heart is the same love that is shown by God to you. Listen to your heart. It is always right. Has your heart ever steered you wrong?

(Yup!)

That depends on how you mean it. I'm sure my heart has steered me to girls I liked who didn't like me back, which broke my heart. I'm sure similar situations have happened to millions of people.

Gabriel: It's always been right, though. Your heart is connected to your instincts. They are intertwined. The love that emanates from your heart is the same love that emanates from your soul. Your soul is connected to your instincts, and therefore, they are the same. Your heart may have loved somebody, but you kind of knew in the back of your mind that they wouldn't feel the same way.

What if they had, though? What if I thought they would never feel the same and they ended up feeling the same way I did? What if my heart loved them, but I had this strong feeling they didn't feel the same—and then they did?

Gabriel: Beau, you always know. Think about that. There are no guessing games or secrets out there except the ones that you create.

(We are creating our own life. I didn't mean to choose that!)

So it's really an instincts game that we are making up?

Gabriel: Life is a game you are making up as you go along. You try, and you either succeed or fail. Trial and error.

Trial and error. T from *trial* plus *error*. Terror. It's Terror going through it.

Gabriel: Look at you, Mr. Wordsmith.

(I'm mentally patting myself on the back.)

I know! I'm so proud of myself. I feel like I was inspired by you to write that.

Gabriel: You are inspired by me to write all of this.

Touché. I guess I am. What else would you like to share with me?

Gabriel: We are going to end this channeling here today. I can give you one more thing, though. It'll be a life lesson: *The cherished ones are everyone, for everyone is cherished.* God cherishes everyone. The Universe cherishes everyone. I cherish everyone. Your soul cherishes everyone. Once you make room in your heart to cherish everyone, life becomes easier because it is so much harder for hate to reside in that space.

(I can share with you from personal experience that having love for everyone, whether or not you like them, makes life so much easier to function in. Remember, you don't have to like people in order to love them or just because you love them.)

Wow, is that powerful! Thank you for sharing that. OK, so if that is the end of this session, I will chat with you again tomorrow morning. Bye, Gabriel!

Gabriel: Bye, Beau. I love you.

Hi, Gabriel. What would you like to share today?

Gabriel: You write your own script. Consider this an expansion of what we just talked about. Do you realize that you have the ability to be 100 percent responsible for your life? This means taking the necessary actions to proceed with the waves of life. It is all your choice. You can choose, think, write down, and then take actions to accomplish everything you want. Life is so simple, but humans get caught up in the web of life.

That makes sense. I tell people all the time that life is easy. We make it hard. Maybe that's easy to say as a young white male.

Gabriel: Thoughts are brought down from generation to generation. You can stop that cycle. It's a choice. Life happens. You must deal with that. It is your choice, however, to react how you choose.

(To me, this goes back to taking 100 percent responsibility for your life. No matter what happens, we make the best of it without letting it affect what we think or how we feel. I get that is so much easier said than done, but I fully believe it. What about you?)

Well, all right. I guess there's no way around that. It is what it is. Why do a majority of humans not truly understand that? It's so easy to make excuses.

Gabriel: This goes back to the fact that it's easier to live in the lower energies. To make excuses. To hate. To have self-doubt. No one *really* wants to live like that, but it's all some know. They think life is meant to be a struggle and to be hard, and so they live that way. What you think, you create. It goes back to life lessons

I taught you. Believe in yourself, and don't take no for an answer. Positivity is the key to the kingdom.

Also, you can be positive and not accomplish what you need to accomplish, if you're still lazy. Realize that generations of storytelling help mold many people into who they are. So many do not follow their dreams. Why do you think you were put on the earth? For God to experience what life is like as you. Wouldn't you want God to experience the best version of you? What about other dimensions, and string theory, which shows other more successful versions of you? What if, instead of one, there were two versions of this successful you? What if you changed dimensions multiple times a day, switching back and forth between the achiever and the dreamer?

Beau, don't get caught up in what you *think* life is. Life is easy. It's really that simple. Stop making life so difficult. Please. It's only doing you injustice. There is not much else to tell you today. Consider what I said, and take it into your life.

Wow. OK, I will Gabriel.

(What sticks out the most, at least to me, is when Archangel Gabriel says, "What if you changed dimensions multiple times a day, switching back and forth between the achiever and the dreamer?" So many of us go through life switching back and forth between achieving our goal and dreaming about our goal. What if we each stayed in the mindset of achieving? This idea of switching between these dimensions is just as much about living out life comfortably. I'm sure we'd all like to live our best life possible. I'm going to challenge myself to that, and I challenge you to do that for you. Let's each take 100 percent responsibility for each of our lives and also for this planet. Game on! Ha!)

Hi, Gabriel. What would you like to share with me this morning?

Gabriel: You know the words from Genesis "Let there be light"? Take those words literally and know that every waking moment of your life is meant to be bright. Light. Bright. **B**ring **L**ove.

Light Bright? Like the toy Lite-Brite, back when I was a kid?

Gabriel: You can look at it like that, yes. The serendipitous ways of being that you possess can be translated into a form that we call Love. Your bright light outline is like your aura. It expands far beyond you, and know that you are the only one who can keep it shining. Your soul works on autopilot, like your heart and brain do. Your whole body works that way. It's how you can move your arms without thinking of all the things your muscles have to do to make it move. You can just decide to lift up your arm, and so it is.

(I never looked at it like that. Wow! There are times the human body blows my mind.)

Well, what about people who are handicapped and cannot move certain body parts. Are you saying they aren't smart enough to do that?

Gabriel: What I am saying is that actions taken by a handicapped person will proceed to launch the Universe into another realm. Some souls have chosen to experience life with those handicaps, and you can't judge them for that. That is how they chose to experience life. Others proceed to follow their own rules once they get here, through accidents and actions. Time heals all wounds. This is not meant literally, but emotionally. You learn to live with what you have, just like you're living with this gift of channeling. Not everyone has it, Beau, just like not everyone is handicapped.

I feel like this conversation doesn't make sense.

Gabriel: On the contrary. Let me prove my point to you. When you stop thinking so much about the consequences of your actions, you will see why God has given you the opportunity to live life by choice. The conversations you have with yourself are conversations you have with God. Since you and God are the same, you are having conversations with yourself. Since you are having conversations with yourself, you are choosing your life moment by moment. Since you are choosing your life moment by moment, you are choosing what it looks like—how you react to certain things.

There is a motivational speaker out there with no arms and no legs. He is a *motivational speaker*. He chose his life the way he wanted to live. He is married and has a child. He chose his life. He was born without limbs, and he decided that wouldn't stop him from living a powerful life. He used his handicap to express to other people that you can overcome anything. You can't even see me, and yet you are typing all of this out with trust and clarity you really hadn't experienced prior.

Use that speaker as an example, for no matter what life throws at you, it's your *choice* as to how you react. He reacted fearlessly and powerfully. Roadblocks got in his way, and he still did what he had to do with no arms and no legs. Life is a journey. Are you going to take the easy way or the hard way? Success is down the hard way. Achieving success is rarely easy. You have to work. This goes back to taking 100 percent responsibility for your life. Motivate yourself. Follow your heart and be fearless.

That is so much easier said than done.

Gabriel: Life is a choice. Laugh along the way. It'll make it easier and more enjoyable during those times when it seems impossible to keep going. Look inside yourself for the answers. They are there.

Look inside myself, as in trust my instincts and heart?

Gabriel: To an extent, yes. You also intuitively know everything and what is best for you and your situation.

So then why do we make it so difficult?

Gabriel: There is something called free will. I am not here to tell you how to live your life. That's a choice. That goes back again to 100 percent responsibility. Once you take 100 percent responsibility, that's when you officially align with God and things start happening. It works every time. The most successful people in the world take 100 percent responsibility for their lives—and voilà.

You make it sound so easy.

Gabriel: When you get rid of fear, you can take 100 percent responsibility. You own up to *everything*. The path to light is the path to love. This is why your light should be bright. The road to success is long and hard. It can also get dark, which is why your light should shine bright. It'll be easier to make it to the end if it is. Some people get stuck in the dark and walk back to where they started.

Wow. You just brought it back to what you said at the beginning. I'm impressed!

Gabriel: I am you. Don't forget that. We're all One. You are creating this conversation for a reason. You needed to hear this. So does the world.

Is there anything else you want to share about this topic?

Gabriel: I have given you everything there is to know about 100 percent responsibility. We shall proceed tomorrow.

Well, OK then. Bye, Gabriel!

(I was clear about it two and a half years ago, and I'm still clear that taking 100 percent responsibility is the most important step in creating the life we want. It's that important and basic a concept. I also get that it is so much *easier said than done. I am going to take this on and see what happens.)*

Hi, Orion and Gabriel. Orion, did I understand you correctly that this will be the last time I channel you for this book?

Orion: Yes. Know that everything I tell you and have told you is there for you to publish for the world, for everything I've shared with you is magical and fruitful. Know that the world is ready for this information. All you have to do is put it out there. It will spread like wildfire. Listen to these words. They are magically delicious.

Are you saying these words are similar to a bowl of Lucky Charms, Orion?

Orion: I use such terms to make you laugh. I hope it is working.

It is. Anyway, what would you like to share with me for this final channeling?

Orion: The time has come for you and the world to activate the dynamic systems of clarity. The time has also come for the world and the universe to open up to the idea that God does in fact exist. The time is now and only now. There is no past and there is no future for you to worry about. Focus on the *Now*. If there is anything I can leave you with, it is that. Be aware that only you are in control of life. Not me. Not God. Not others. It is just you. That is the hardest thing for humans to grasp. You attract, create, and birth *everything* that happens to you. Remember that.

(This is where 100 percent responsibility comes in. We are the creators of our life through and through.)

What can you share about the universe? Any new insight?

Orion: Everything and everyone is connected. I am you. I am the forest. I am the spaceship I travel in. *You* are the spaceship I travel in. *You* are the forest. We are all connected. Do you get the point I am trying to make to you, Beau? The longevity of the earth is completely translated into thoughts and ideas and life that you and the human race create. There are no mistakes. There are only opportunities to make a better life. The thoughts and ideas that surround the planet surround each of you individually.

The time has come for you to realize that you are calm and collected energy beings. However, you have the free will to choose your final outcome in life. There will be a time in your lives when you realize that the only one who made decisions was you. Most people see it happen in their old age. Once they've gone through everything and they go through a life review before they cross over, they realize that there were so many things they could have done differently. Don't let that happen. Go after your dreams. You only live in this life you are currently living once. You will return in different forms in different lives. This particular life, though, you only live once. Make it count.

Wow. That was powerful. Thank you for that reminder, Orion. Is there anything else you'd like to share on this final channeling?

Orion: I will return for other channelings for other reasons. Be great, Beau. There is nothing else left to share.

All right, Gabriel, would you like to chime in with anything?

Gabriel: Yes, I would. Be creation. Be powerful. Be yourself. Be you.

Easy enough. Anything else?

Gabriel: Take these lessons into the world. Be great, Beau. You are walking with God at all times.

Because God is everywhere?

Gabriel: Know that the time has come for you to realize that the causation of truth is within you.

Wait. We cause truth?

Gabriel: It is all perception *and* you are God in human form. If that is so, then you created Truth. It may sound far-fetched, but know that if you are God in human form, then yes, you created, or caused, Truth.

(This is just more reassurance that we create our lives through and through.)

Talk about abstract.

Gabriel: Life is not abstract. The truth is the truth is the truth. The Universe only understands and exists through truth. The Universe is not lying about the trees and the color of the leaves. They are the colors they are. Trees look how they look. There is a truth within them. You caused it and are *causing* it. You see, Beau, you conceive reality in how you see the world.

I watched this movie that talked like this. We create the world, but more on an individual basis. It's how we perceive it. Am I even close to explaining that correctly?

Gabriel: Yes, you are. The world is viewed through perception. The world is your creation. *You* are your own creation. You get to choose who you are. Therefore, you as a race get to choose how the planet looks, figuratively and literally. Wars only happen by choice.

("Wars only happen by choice" is such a strong but truthful statement.)

But natural disasters don't. They just happen.

Gabriel: Mother Nature exists as her own entity, and she does what she has to do to survive and reacts the way she reacts to protect herself from harm. These things that happen to her that make her react in certain ways to keep herself safe are created by the human race. Therefore, you are helping create that. You see, when your body fights off dis-ease, it does what it has to do to survive. The same thing goes for the earth. Mother Nature does what she has to do. If there are poisonous toxins being distributed amongst her beauty, she will safeguard herself.

The human body does the same. Why do you think you feel nauseous when you're sick? Something is off-balance. Why does your body react the way it does to fight off dis-ease or viruses? It is protecting itself. You throw up or sneeze and heal to protect yourself. The human body is a reflection of Mother Nature.

This is getting deep, Gabriel. I'd ask why you're telling me this, but I think it's to point out and remind me that not only is everything connected and One, but also to remind me that we are reflections of each other. If I am the Universe in human form, then it only makes sense I am the Earth in human form, being that we're all One.

Gabriel: I am glad you see this. That is the whole point. Treat yourself the best way you can. Treat Mother Nature the best way you can. The only difference is that you have to convince other people of this news. You are like the cells of the planet Earth. You treat the planet Earth well, and it will show its love right back. You are literally feeding each other. You and Mother Nature have a symbiotic relationship. Don't ever forget that.

(Treat the Earth right. Treat it how you want to be treated. I hope that's with love and appreciation.)

I never even looked at it like that. I mean, I saw how the earth was reacting to what we were doing to it, but I never looked at it like how you just explained, nor do I really ever consider that I am the Earth in human form. I knew I was the Universe in human form, but I never considered myself to be the Earth, too. Is there anything else you'd like to share?

Gabriel: That is all for now. Take this information into the world at your earliest convenience and share it.

I will. Bye, Gabriel.

Gabriel: Until next time, right?

Ha, yes. Until next time.

Good morning, Gabriel. What would you like to share this morning?

Gabriel: Know that everything I share with you is dictation about the lives that you currently aren't living, for the human race is living more so off of ego than it is trust of the Universe. The paradigm shift that is taking place upon the planet will soon reach enough people that the planes of dimensions and truth will shift and you will be in a new world of love and prosperity.

Know that climate change is coming, and it will only encourage you to be the best you can be. The chosen ones will emerge into one big love and share with the planet what it has been missing for a long time: clarity. It is happening with a lot of you, but it is not happening enough for the thoughts and ideas of heaven on earth to tilt.

There is also the Law of Dichotomy, which is meant to enhance the difference between *good* and *bad*. Please remember that there are no such things as good and bad. It is merely a choice of observation. What is good to you may be bad to someone else and vice versa. Don't be too caught up in the fabrication of lies that lie upon your thoughts collectively. Know that the only one judging is you. The time will soon emerge when the difference between good and bad will be realized more as a choice than an absolute.

That was the most profoundly I think you've ever spoken to me. You usually sound more lighthearted and fun. That was straightforward.

Gabriel: Remember that how you hear me is a choice. It's all a choice. Choices create outcomes create observations create more choices. "How should I take this?" "Why did they say that?" "What they said reminds me so much of my mom!" Realize that everything you see, do, and hear is filtered by the lenses you wear throughout your life.

People are affected differently by the same outcome. Don't read too much into anything. The clarity that follows you is kept deep within the mind. The advantageous ways of life are showing up right now, and know that every millisecond of your life is created through choice. The lenses that you wear are prescribed for *your* sight only. No one on the planet has the same prescription. Do you understand this?

I do. We *all* see the world differently.

(If we can realize that we all see the world differently, then nobody should be mad when someone else doesn't see what we do, no matter how obvious it is to us.)

Gabriel: And because of that, the world will never be exactly how *you* want it or see it. There need to be (and always will be) different collections of outlooks amongst everyone.

What does all this mean? Why are you telling me this?

Gabriel: The keen eye of your soul is realizing that life is not as easy as it appears. Let me express this more clearly: Life itself is easy. The *universe* is what is complex. The way it operates. The way it moves. The ways of being are easy to figure out but tough to understand for most.

Can you explain this with more clarity? I think I get your point, but I feel it would be easier to understand if it were further simplified.

Gabriel: The only one judging yourself and your intelligence is you. I want you to know that. Here it is in simpler terms: You create. You make choices. You observe and then decide. It's really as easy as that. Once the planet understands that, Life as you know it will be easier for a lot of you to walk through.

I know I might sound judging, but it is only because I am coming through with more clarity and you have let your guard down some and started to trust more of what I am sharing with you. You made it easier to read at the beginning because your mind and brain decided to simplify it. That is all. The walls are coming down, and know that you are watching them fall. The walls you once had up are turning into crumbling bricks, and you can now see and hear me with more clarity. Don't be afraid or worried. I am still the same loving and fun Gabriel you've always known.

(Based on every conversation I've had with Archangel Gabriel over the past few years, here's what I feel Gabriel means regarding all of this: Life is easy. We make it hard. Another way of saying this is that life is easy, but it is hard for us as human beings to fully understand. This is why we don't always understand why things happen the way they do. There are so many ways of learning a lesson, which we signed up to learn before our soul came to Earth to live the life we're in, and the lesson will keep repeating until we learn it. Even explaining this makes me question so much about life, and I wonder if I'm pointing everything out. I feel I'm not, but I do feel I'm sharing the basics, and that is enough.)

Thank you for clearing that up. I feel better. Is there anything else you'd like to share with me?

Gabriel: There is nothing else for this morning's channeling.

Good evening, Gabriel. Will you please explain in further detail the sentence I heard recently, "Absolute composure is the measurement of absolute suffering?"

Gabriel: Yes, I'd love to. Here it is. "Composure"—let us explain this piece in further detail. *Composure* is another way of saying your state of being. Are you composed? Are you put together? Are you here in your full capacity? If you are here and alive on this earth, then the answer is yes. The absolute composure that resides in your cerebellum is the truth in human form. There is no mistake when I tell you that your brain is the part of you that physically expresses and develops emotion on a molecular level. There is no wrong way for this to occur.

(A heads-up that this may get confusing. Stay with me here. I explain this clearly at the end.)

We can then go to "the measurement of absolute suffering." The way that the mind and brain work is a symbiotic relationship of molecules and certainty. The way that the soul is connected is a transfer of energy between the body and the mind. Here you have it that absolute suffering is not being connected both spiritually to God and physically to your brain. When you are in a conduction of misconduct amongst yourself, you are therefore in absolute suffering. Your idea of composure doesn't exist in this world.

So, if absolute composure is the measurement of absolute suffering, then how can they be connected if they aren't existing in the same realm? Easy, for one is a product of the other. Your composure can create your suffering. The point I am trying to make here is that the serendipitous movement of the mind is translated into the equilibrium.

(What I feel this all means is that how you feel emotionally will dictate how you feel physically, and vice versa. If you don't feel good about yourself, even subconsciously, then it will be reflected in how you function physically and also in terms of what you attract. Archangel Gabriel explains it in simpler terms below.)

Gabriel, I had to stop and read that because I was getting confused, and it stopped making sense to me. Can you describe this more clearly, please?

Gabriel: What I want you to get is that composure and suffering are opposites, and yet one cannot exist without the other. If there was no composure, then there would be no frame of reference for suffering. They are opposites but connected, and they are mirrors of each other. Be composed absolutely through and through.

At the moment, you are not [composed], you are suffering. One cannot exist without the other, and yet they can't exist within the same space. That is all. The point of me telling you this is for you to know that this is what life is like. This is how manifestation works. This is how life works. This happens to you, Beau, all the time. You want something, yet if there is something else just like it taking up a certain area of your life, then that other thing can't exist until the original thing is gone.

For example, if you spend time talking to someone about a romantic partner you want and there is no room for an actual girlfriend, then the new partner can't show up in your world. Once room is made, they will show up. Absolute composure is having the thing you want. Absolute suffering is not having it and complaining about it. Being sad. Produce the results you want by making room for it. It's really that easy.

(Look at composure and suffering as you would love and hate: Though they are opposites, one can't exist without the other. If it weren't for hate, we wouldn't really know how love looked and felt. We wouldn't really know what good was without bad. We wouldn't know what composure truly was without suffering, and yet they can't exist in the same space. You can't be composed but still be suffering. That doesn't make sense, just as you can't love somebody and hate them at the same time.)

Thank you for clearing that up. Is there anything else?

> **Gabriel:** No, Beau. There is nothing else for you for this channel. Have a great sleep, Beau.

Hello, Gabriel. How are you?

> **Gabriel:** Beau, I am great. It is time to get to your next question. Your dreams and desires are the actions of your life. This really goes back to the concept of 100 percent responsibility. Take the action you want to take to make your dreams and desires your reality. No one else is going to do this for you. Not God. Not I. Not your mother. Not your children. *You* and only you. Others can assist, but the end result is created by your actions and your actions only.
>
> Be aware that blaming other people makes you small. There is no need for that way of being. That your dreams and desires result from the actions of your life is another way of saying that those dreams and actions are part of the journey to where you want to be. Don't ever indulge in actions that do not take you down the path of absolute satisfaction. Be One with God on your journey. You can also say this as "Be One with Your Self." When you are able to manifest your ideas into reality, that is when things begin to change. Acknowledge your purpose and trek on to greener pastures.

What a marvelous way of saying that. That was really just a long way of saying "Take 100 percent responsibility for your life."

> **Gabriel:** And know that all there is to do is realize that God Itself created everything to *create* everything. God has help and assistance from other things he created, yet God was the one who created everything. Do you understand this?

I do. God may have had assistance in helping create everything, but it was God that took that 100 percent responsibility in seeing everything to completion. So are you trying to point out how important teamwork is?

Gabriel: What I want to point out is that the colleagues who help you were created by your thoughts and actions. Dreams are thoughts. Your dreams and actions created [your life]. People and things showed up to help you create what you saw in your mind. God did the same thing to create everything. You are God in human form. It's really that simple, Beau. Don't complicate the obvious.

I wouldn't exactly call that obvious, for I don't think everyone knows that or thinks that way.

Gabriel: Who's to say that you have to believe it for it to be true? Truth is truth whether you believe it or not. You are typing all of this on your laptop right now. Someone can believe that you're typing this on a typewriter with all of their heart. The truth is that you're typing this on your computer. There is nothing else to say here. The truth is the truth.

I get the concept you are making. Is there anything else you'd like to share about all of this?

Gabriel: There is only this: Know you are *fully* responsible for *everything* that happens to you. *Period.* While you have certain obligations to fulfill, you are in control of how you fulfill those obligations. The truth will set you free, Beau. Truly and truthfully. Take 100 percent responsibility for your life and see what happens when you do. You'll be floored.

I've known of people who did this, and they are wealthy beyond belief and *happy*. They are where they want to be, and they did it on their own terms. It's really as simple as that.

Gabriel: So model your life after theirs. Copy them and their ways of being. They always came from a place of Peace. I've said that to you before. God is Peace. *You* are Peace. Not everyone realizes that, but it is true. You are everything, so you *have* to be

Peace. Once you can align yourself and soul with the Peace within you, you will see the results come at you tenfold. I love you all with all my soul and spirit and being.

I love you, too, and I'm sure everyone who knows you exist loves you. Is there anything else you'd like to share?

Gabriel: Just know that the world is created by you and everyone else. God just experiences. The earth retaliates. Period.

I would think the Earth only retaliates when actions are brought against it. Not when things that are good are done to it.

Gabriel: All the earth is doing is living and surviving. That's it.

This is just a whole other discussion we're about to get into. All I ask is that you make this explanation short and sweet.

Gabriel: No problem. First is not to take the word *retaliate* literally. The word *retaliate* is also known as good in this instance. If the earth is treated well, it will thank you. If the earth is treated badly, it will euthanize what was just done to it to survive. Does this make sense to you?

(I see Gabriel using the word retaliate *more as* responds. *For example, "The word* retaliate *is also known as good in this instance." It is retaliating, or rather responding, with a thank-you when treated well.)*

Yes, it does. Thank you. Is there anything else?

Gabriel: That is it for today. Enjoy yourself, and remember: You are God in human form. God is everything and is the creator of everything. You are the same. Be well.

You as well.

Good afternoon, Gabriel. It is great to connect with you on this lovely afternoon.

Gabriel: And you too. It is always a pleasure, Beau. Let's get started. The measurement of your life is successful actions. I'm going to take you right back to our conversation about 100 percent responsibility. This requires action on your part. Massive action. What you want to appear in your world will not happen by wishing alone. Take action. Learn along the way. The more you learn and the more you implement what you learn will help you take successful actions.

The prognosis of defeat is directed by the temperament of your soul. If you feel you are a failure, then that is what your soul will think, which is what your thoughts will create, which will create the actions you take. One thing leads to another. It is a domino effect. Now, you can easily be down on yourself and take action—and take *successful* actions on top of that. Let's say you achieve what you want. If you're down and out about yourself, you will not be able to enjoy that success. Same goes with the rest of life. If you're looking for a romantic partner, then you will attract someone of the same caliber who is also down and out about their life. That would be a miserable relationship, wouldn't it? Be happy. Be positive as much as you possibly can because when the greatness rolls around, you should enjoy it. Being sad while achieving success doesn't make much sense, does it?

(This sounds like the Law of Attraction. What you put out you get back.)

No, it doesn't. Great point made. Does this also mean to believe in yourself and know that your actions will lead you to what you want to achieve?

Gabriel: Absolutely, it does! Be aware that success is a choice and a state of mind. Those who have lived a life that has brought them down can achieve success just as well as someone with a more enthusiastic way of being and [an] "easier" life. Remember, hard and easy are outlooks. There is no right or wrong, so there is no hard and easy. What's hard to you could be easy to someone else.

Remember this. Bring those into your life who will be able to do things better than you can, but only if you choose to do that. Life is a choice. That again goes back to the idea of 100 percent responsibility. The journey of life begins now and has no end until you decide to create one. Everything about your life, you make up. The things that happen, the way you look at things, and much more. You are a creating machine. Know this for the future.

I thought there was no future?

Gabriel: When I say *future,* I do not mean that in literal terms. The future is right now, and it is also the past. Life is happening *now* and *only* now. That last sentence is now the past, and this part you're typing was the future ten seconds ago. Do you see what I mean? Are you getting it?

(A brilliant way of reminding us that there is only Now.)

I am. Life only exists *now.* Take 100 percent responsibility *now.*

Gabriel: Remember that life is *your* choice and *only you* can create your life how you want. You can be told this concept and even understand it, but if you don't take these lessons into action, then it is just a lesson learned. You know it intellectually but not literally in your physical universe. That's why God made Life. It understood *everything* for *ever,* and knowing is just half the battle. Life was created so God could *experience* what It understood. Do you get that?

Absolutely, and that is why we are God in human form.

Gabriel: Right. Let us be clear, it is just one sliver of why you are God in human form, but it is a big part of it.

Is there anything else you'd like to share about this lesson?

Gabriel: That is all there is. We will be moving out of the conversation about 100 percent responsibility at the next channeling we do.

I am excited! Bye, Gabriel.

Gabriel: Good-bye, Beau.

Hello, Gabriel! Good morning.

Gabriel: Hi, Beau. Good morning to you. Let's get started on this next message: *Humans like to intellectualize everything.* This really couldn't be simpler. Human beings like to overthink everything, and there is no need for this. Many of you think that nothing happens after death. Of those who do think something happens, some think of it so much differently than others. *Heaven* is a concept only. There is absolutely a life after death, for your spirit returns home to the other side—but it doesn't mean that there is a heaven as described in the Bible and other books.

Know that the truth is setting you free. The obstacles that get in your way are the same ones that get in the way of everything. This comes right back around to overintellectualizing everything. I've said before that life is so simple. Stop making things more difficult than they are. There is no need. You are a spiritual being having a physical experience. When you pass away from the earth, your spirit returns home. It returns back to the Everything. It returns back to the All. There is really no easier way to say this.

You are Spirit first and foremost. God is Spirit energy. *Everything* is energy, and until you understand this, you will intellectualize everything. Once you become clear that we are all One, you will begin to realize how silly it is to intellectualize life and spirit. There is no common denominator except energy. God is energy. *You* are energy. You are God in human form. I say this with Love, Beau. I want to be very clear about this message because the world isn't getting it on a large enough scale.

(This is such an important message for us to get. This is also not meant to discredit the Bible. If that's what you believe, that's great. Archangel

Gabriel is saying that the other side is not how it is described—it's even better. I am very clear that God/the Universe is not judgmental.)

It really keeps going back to the same message that we are all One. We should stop intellectualizing everything. It is much simpler than we're making it.

> **Gabriel:** Know this: You are all loved equally. How is that possible? You are God. You are God's children. You are part of this great energy that you call "God." God is not some big man in the sky waiting to judge you at the gates of Heaven. God is love, a love you can't really understand as a human being. This doesn't make you stupid. That's a concept. You are *all* brilliant, and I wish you could all see that. There is no "stupid" or "dumb" or "slow." This is a stamp put on people by society. What is "dumb" to you may be brilliant to someone else. Life is a choice. It is all about your view. Observe life, but don't let it define things for you.

(This is a reminder that we as humans are smarter than we give ourselves credit for.)

Talk about deep. Again, it's the same messages in different words. Am I wrong?

> **Gabriel:** Life is a choice. Life is determined by your outlook on it. All there is, is energy and observation. *That's it.* Why overanalyze Life? What is the reason behind this? Human beings were given the freedom to think freely, so questioning everything is completely OK. However, I am here to tell you that there is no need for this. Have belief. Have faith. Just because it doesn't exist in plain view in the way you expect it to look, doesn't mean it doesn't exist. *God is all around you,* but there are enough of you on this planet who think differently. Some of you are expecting a person to show up and tell you he is God or Jesus. If that person appeared, he would be persecuted and thrown in a mental ward. Am I wrong?

You're absolutely right. If God or Jesus came to earth in the form of a human being and showed his true power, he would be locked up.

> **Gabriel:** That's exactly how it would happen—or worse. There are "crazy" people that show up on the news and are looked at as "weird." Beau, I tell you this: Human beings intellectualize everything. That's all that is there to understand. God bless.

I guess that's the end of this channeling?

> Yes. I have shared all there is for this message.

Good afternoon, Gabriel! How are you?

Gabriel: Oh, Beau. I am wonderful as always. Would you like to get started? I know you'd like to do two lessons to make up for not channeling me yesterday. We can do that.

(Around this time, I began receiving more "lessons." They'd come through while I was, say, watching television, and I'd type some notes in my phone to ask Gabriel about in our next channel.)

Yes. It looks like the next lesson is: *The value isn't in the money. The value is in cherishing the moments of life.* Can you please explain more about this lesson?

Gabriel: Always, in all ways. The value of life is definitely not in the money. It is *definitely* in the moments of life. You cannot bring money with you when you leave your earthly body and come over to the other side. You can, however, bring memories, for memories are what are displayed during your Life Review. There is no winner in terms of who earned the most money. Of course, many human beings want a lot of money. More of them, though, just want to be comfortable.

In your country of America, money runs everything. In other countries, there is not as much greed running rampant when it comes to money. However, everyone wants and deserves to be happy and to be able to maintain themselves financially.

Let's look more into this. Haven't you noticed that people in other countries who don't have a lot of anything are usually the happiest? It is a choice. That is all they know, and so all that's left is choice. There is no option for a "better" life in some parts of the world. They work with what they have and look at life through those eyes. It is all about interpretation. It is all about feeling and choice—and *not* about money.

Money is a freedom some people have and a lot of people don't. Live your life how you want to live your life, for your memories and the moments of life will always conquer the lust you have for money and comfort. There are people you would consider poor who are happier than you are. That's how the world is.

Talk about deep! I do know people who don't have much when it comes to money but who are living their dreams. I've even met people who are living the life I've always dreamed of and who are scraping by financially but couldn't be happier. It is definitely a choice.

Gabriel: Just like the rest of life. I will always remind you that life is a choice.

Please continue. I could use that reminder once in a while. Is that everything you'd like to share on that subject? Can I move to the next lesson?

Gabriel: Yes, you can, for that is all there is regarding what you asked about. Let's get right into it: *The outer essence of your being is the inner essence of your seeing.* We can connect this lesson to the last. Who you are on the outside is who you are on the inside. Some people feel awful about themselves yet present themselves as happy and cheerful on the outside. That is a mask and not the real them. This goes back to the lesson, *Be a bridge for others.* Let others be a bridge for you. Stop hiding from life if you don't like how your life looks. People want to help. [Most] people are nice. However, some people don't know how to be nice with others, and those are the people who are wearing a mask.

Wait a minute . . . what about terrorists and people who go out and commit murder and bloodshed because they think *their* God is more important and better than anyone else's God?

Gabriel: This is a choice that people make, and those people are wearing a mask and may not even realize it. They are also coming from a place of fear. Again, people, at their core, are nice. They are sweet and loving and just want the best for people. Some of those people think the best for everyone else is going to be the same as what they think is the best for them. Do you get this? War is a choice.

How in the world is war a choice for the people getting bombed, who have no choice about living in that and have to run for their lives?

Gabriel: Here we go with the intellectualizing everything. Life is a choice, Beau. Some souls sign up for this kind of life in their lifetime. Free will. Choice. It's all about experience. Happiness. Sadness. It is all a choice *no matter what* is happening around you.

There was the person who wrote a book about himself and his child being in the middle of the Holocaust, who turned hiding from the Nazis into a game with his son so his son wouldn't become scared. Do you understand what I am getting at? It is a choice. He realized he could either run scared with his child or he could turn it into a game and make it livable and fun.

People have a choice. Nelson Mandela was in jail for most of his life. Yet, it was his choice how he lived through it. They captured his body but not his mind. A true warrior of life was Nelson Mandela.

Life is a choice. Once you get this concept, you will realize how amazing life really is no matter what is happening around you. There are people who will argue this, and it may be easier said than done. Life is a choice. How you live it is a choice. Happiness is a choice. Choose love. Love will always triumph.

I definitely see the point you're trying to make. I'm just thinking about people I know who will more than likely disagree with that.

(Simply put, life is a choice, and there are certain situations we as souls sign up for to experience. Some souls choose to be born into a war zone to experience that kind of life. Some souls choose to be born into riches to experience that kind of life. There are so many different options that our souls can choose to take, and life can be very overwhelming to us as human beings. It may not even make sense. It's simply a decision our soul makes more for us to experience as humans, and we have free will as humans to choose how we will respond.)

Gabriel: And if they disagree, that is a *choice*. Do you get that?

Yes, I can get that. It still seems easier said than done, though.

Gabriel: It is easier for human beings to live in the lower level of negativity. When the planet realizes that life and *everything* about life is a choice, the world will be at so much more peace. Love. Love. Love.

I don't even know where to go from here.

Gabriel: What I want you to get is that being happy is definitely easier said than done. You are living a life free of bloodshed and war and worrying about your next meal. It is easier to be happy, right? Not really. It is a choice. There are those, as I mentioned, who have next to nothing and always have a smile on their face. They are not letting money be the determining factor in their life. There are people who are rich beyond the lives of most who are sad and miserable. It's a choice.

Great point made. Is there anything else?

Gabriel: Be happy.

I will do my best to remain that way no matter what is happening in my life because I now really know that it is a choice. Thank you, Gabriel.

Gabriel: You are welcome. Be bold. Be encouraging. Be peaceful and respectful to others and especially yourself.

Gabriel, are you there?

Gabriel: I am always here with you. Remember that I and God have given you this gift of channel. Use it well. Benefit from it. Take it into your life like you've been doing and watch the magic happen. The things I teach you always work. Don't hesitate.

Got it. I will continue. So I saw the next lesson is: *Beware of your passions, for they can haunt you if you don't act upon them.* Please explain this in further detail, Gabriel.

Gabriel: Absolutely, I will. This is self-explanatory; it is really a simple concept and explanation. You should understand this personally, Beau, for I know you've dealt with this through a lot of your life, regarding what you are most passionate about. Let's get into further detail of this lesson, though.

If you don't chase after your dreams, then you will never see them formulate into reality. If you never accomplish your goals (as in, you never take any action to achieve them), then they will become regrets when you get older. There are so many people out there in old age—or just old enough that it's too late to accomplish what they dreamed of as a kid—who carry such huge regrets about all the things they never did. Know that this can happen to you or anybody.

Anyone can accomplish victory in their life, but victory is not meant for certain people. Now, I don't want you to get discouraged when you don't end up where you thought you would in the chase of the greatest life you can imagine. It will still be great. It just may not look the way you expect it to look sometimes. People get caught up in the glitz and glamour and forget that the way to a happy life and success is following your dreams to *be happy*. To be the best you.

Some people out there get caught up in fame and forget why they started their journey in the first place. Beau, I am glad you know better yourself. Lots of people don't, and it especially happens in youth. Sometimes, people accomplish success quickly, before they get to know themselves. Don't let such a thing cripple you. See, people who achieve major success when they're young can do things along the way that they will regret in old age—maybe even sooner if it majorly affects their life. Don't get caught in the *wow*. Stay in the Now and be present and alive. Don't be moving through life as if you're better than everyone else. Everyone is *equally* great. Love. Be that. Be Love.

(Archangel Gabriel is saying that we should follow our dreams to be happy. It doesn't mean that living the dream itself will make us happy. We may get there and be sad, in which case, we usually either adjust to make things happy for ourselves or realize that no matter what, we aren't going to be happy, so we go in a new direction. I have a feeling this happens often, but we don't always adjust if need be. If we do, it may be in a direction we didn't even consider originally.)

That makes absolute sense. Some people out there . . .

Gabriel: *Most* people out there . . .

I get your point. *Most* people out there don't appreciate success for what it really is. Some let it go to their head. Some are still miserable. This goes back to life being a choice. Is this what you're trying to point to?

Gabriel: Not really. That's a great observation, though. Remember this, if anything, from this conversation: Take on life and get what you want. When you get what you want, acknowledge it, celebrate it, be happy, and then move on to a new goal. Keep yourself in motion. Don't *ever* stop. Remember, Beau: Life is all about momentum.

(Wow, that's powerful. That's a whole new way to look at life.)

Indeed, it is. Is there anything else you'd like to share regarding this lesson?

Gabriel: That is all for now. There will be more in due time.

That's great to know. Can I ask about the next lesson?

Gabriel: Yes.

Great. The next lesson you had given me was: *The coward who shoots the arrow is the one who gets hurt the most.* I really don't get this one, so I'd love to see how you explain this.

Gabriel: It is quite simple, really. Don't overanalyze this. Ready? The concept of life is to remember that you are all equal. This means that you are reflections of each other. When the coward shoots the arrow of hurtful words or actions, he is daring. Also remember that he is shooting this arrow with fear and out of fear. It may hurt someone. Most of the time it does because he's so fearful that fear gets put into the tip of that arrow. His cowardly ways pierce those who are fearless or not expecting the arrow. It catches those off guard and hurts those people. The hurt those people have is then given right back to him through complaints, responses, doses of anger, frustration.

There is nothing "wrong" with this. Remember that when you do things out of fear, it can sometimes and usually [does] lead to a fear-based result. You do things out of hesitance with a twist of fault. There is never a "good" way to shoot an arrow of fear. Also remember that being a "coward" is truly a choice. You are not born a coward. There is no physical thing called "coward." All it is, is a label you gave yourself or someone else gave to you. If you shoot this arrow out of fear because you feel you are a coward, then that fear will translate into what is used to pierce and sink in to those people or things that are attacked. Love life, Beau. Be fearless.

(Know that your actions and words can be hurtful and sometimes damaging to the person they are aimed at. Even if their words/actions are hurtful to you, do your best to rise above and not do that right back, even if they started it. I know this is much easier said than done in some cases. Let karma handle it.)

That is easier said than done for most people.

Gabriel: Life and living it by choice is also easier said than done, and yet people do it. Don't ever evaluate your fears as paralyzing effects.

(In other words, don't ever be stopped by fear.)

I don't know how to respond.

Gabriel: Let's go to the next lesson, for it will further explain this: *Trepidation is the key to successful things.* The more you watch your steps, the easier it is to be successful heading down the road you're heading. There is a difference between a coward and the word *trepidation*.

When you read the definitions of *trepidation* and *coward,* you see that trepidation is more of a feeling or hint of fear. It's also a way of saying "be careful." The definition of *coward* is "someone *who is* fearful and acts *out* of fear." Just because you have a *feeling* of fear at the moment doesn't necessarily make you a coward. You can jump out of a plane with trepidation. You still do it, though, and by your own choice. A coward either (a) wouldn't even get *on* the plane to jump off it or (b) would be talked *onto* the plane and end up being too scared to jump—and either wouldn't jump *out* of fear or would be *pushed out* and fall down to the ground *in* fear. There is so much difference.

Athletes do things with trepidation. People who are known to have tremendous courage do things with trepidation but still do those things, no matter what. They don't let that fear get in their way of accomplishment. Cowards wouldn't even do those things. They would let their fear overpower them.

How is that related to the arrow?

Gabriel: We can say it like this: The person who is doing things in trepidation may do things out of fear but still do those things anyway. Things change the dynamic every time in terms of how the outcome is created. A coward shoots the arrow in fear and expects a fearful ending, so that is what is created. He didn't even want to shoot the arrow to begin with. He may not have even paid attention to how or where he shot it, so there is a much better chance of the arrow landing poorly. At least the person who did it with trepidation did it smartly and paid attention.

(Imagine if we lived in trepidation instead of being scared to do whatever it is. We can be careful and aware of the dangers, so we prepare ourselves the best we can and then do what we fear anyway. There have been so many times in my life I've been too afraid to do something and missed the opportunity completely to accomplish it. Don't let that happen to you—I'm not going to let it happen to me anymore.)

This is another level of conversation, Gabriel. I'm really blown away by this.

Gabriel: No need. Let's do the next lesson, for it all ties together. It'll be the last one for this channeling.

So, the next lesson is: *Ingenious effort is proclaimed by those who wait.* Please explain how this lesson ties together with the last two, because I don't see it.

Gabriel: This simply means that waiting gives a person a chance to evaluate the situation. They then can see a clever way to accomplish their goal. They wait and evaluate. Now that they've done this and see a way to accomplish it, they do just that. Once they accomplish it, they can share with people how they accomplished it. They can even explain *how* they are going to accomplish it. They can accomplish it with trepidation. They may have *had* fear, but they (a) did it with confidence and (b) didn't let the fear cripple them. The coward *would* let the fear cripple him. Don't be afraid. Be yourself and be powerful. Be amazing and be smart. It's all a choice, Beau. There, I tied it back in.

Ha! I see what you did there. Well, that was very cool to see how this lesson did, in fact, tie in. Is there anything else you'd like to share?

Gabriel: That's it for tonight. I have shared much tonight.

Yes, you have, and thank you for doing so.

Good morning, Gabriel. Lovely speaking with you last night and again this morning. What would you like to share this morning?

Gabriel: Well, of course I'd like to share the next lesson I gave you, which is: *The aspiration of creativity is demanded by the soul.* There are so many of you who don't follow your hearts. This plays off the last lesson. *Follow your heart.* There is nothing stopping you but yourself.

Creativity is inspired. The angelic realm and God Itself supply you with motivation and ideas to be creative. When you all of a sudden come up with a great idea about how to do something, it was inspired. Take this into consideration: Inspiration is the result of aspiration. You are wishing and hoping for a great result, and then boom! You are inspired. See how that works? Aspire and Inspire. *A* is for All (that's you all) and *I* is for Impossible, Incredible Imagination (that's the angelic realm/God/fifth dimension). You *aspire* and we *inspire*. Do you get that?

Yes, I do. Interesting how you made that work. That seemed a little forced, though, I must admit.

Gabriel: So then let us do it this way: *A* is for *angelic* and *I* is for *everything*. The angelic aspires for you and then I, which is also us, inspires you. We are all One. We are bringing God's ideas to you. God lives vicariously through you. God knows everything. God uses you to experience life and feel/see/hear/touch/taste what it's like to live and be one with knowledge.

(Archangel Gabriel doesn't mean I *as in the letter. It's meant as a Being. For example, I am this. I did that. Gabriel constantly tells me that we are*

everything. *That means that I am everything. This is what Gabriel means by "I is for everything."*)

That was something else. Can we say that the *I* in *inspire* can also represent the word *idea?*

> **Gabriel:** You are getting it. It is clicking for you. Good. You are now getting all of this. Ideas are inspired by the angelic when you aspire.

That is *so* much simpler. Thank you for simplifying it like that.

> **Gabriel:** Anything I can do to help explain life better. All of this is just a game. The easier I can make it for you, the better it will be transmitted.

Is there anything else?

> **Gabriel:** No, that is all.

Hi, Gabriel! It's always a pleasure to channel you.

Gabriel: If you only knew how much joy I get out of coming into your presence to share these life lessons with you.

I had to look at the list of lessons you gave me to know the next one, and it is: *Each acquisition of life is dedicated to the server of the mind.* Please explain this further because I'm trying to figure out what you mean, and I don't think I'm getting it.

Gabriel: Let's say this first. Know that you *can* understand it all and you are choosing not to because you don't think you're smart enough. Decisions, decisions, choices, choices. *Choose* to "get it." *Choose* to be intelligent. It is all a choice, this understanding thing.

(We get to choose to be intelligent? I should have done this before tests in school I didn't study for!)

That is so much easier said than done, Gabriel. How can I easily choose that?

Gabriel: How can you easily choose chocolate cake over vegetable salad? It's a choice. It is as easy as whatever is more important to you. Choices, Beau. That's all life is—choices. Another phrase for *acquisition* is *positive choosing*. The lesson here is to learn that the world is dedicated to your growth, and therefore, it is the spinning globe that works with you to help decide your life.

This is abstract. Can you simplify this, Gabriel?

Gabriel: Of course. Let me say this. Know that you are a creator. The creator creates. The choices you make create your life, correct? So then the skills you are learning are dedicated to the server of the mind. Take the word *server* literally. The skills of life are dedicated to you. *You* are the server of your own mind. God is the server of your own mind. The Universe is the server of your own mind.

Am I getting too deep? You are the server of your mind, right? Good. So know that the skills you are developing serve your mind. That's a very simple way to put it, right? "You are the creator of your own world" is another way of twisting it and making it more accessible. Trust the skills that you learn or have already learned. They are serving you and your mind, for your mind is in turn serving *you*.

(Acquisition *means the development of a skill and* server *means a person or thing that provides a service. Therefore, each development of a skill of life is dedicated to the service of the mind. So the skills we develop in life help us get through life. Those skills we learn alter our mind.*)

That is a bit easier to get. I didn't expect it to come back around to the idea of choices, though. Everything is the same, Gabriel. I keep expecting this really deep and amazing lesson that is brand-new to me, something I never thought about. Yet it always leads back to the same stuff. I know I've said it a million times before, but I crave brand-new information.

Gabriel: Are you ready, then? We can go right to the next lesson.

The next lesson I have is: *Life can be channeled through your thoughts and ideas.* What can you share about that?

Gabriel: What I can share is that this universe is not complicated, nor is it really easy to understand. It is beyond your thought process, and yet it is as simple to understand as how to blow a bubble. Love is all there is, Beau. If we broke everything down to its finest particle, that particle would be love. *Evol.* See how *love* backwards almost looks like the word *evil?* There's a difference.

The *i* in *evil* represents just one person. The word *love* backwards has an *o* in place of the *i*. The *o* is a full circle, meaning that we are all One. *I* is separate. *O* is everyone. Everything. That's why it is love. Are you understanding this?

(I would like to share what I feel is meant by "this universe is not complicated, nor is it really easy to understand." What I believe this means is that the universe can be figured out by scientists who study space, but it doesn't always make total sense why things operate the way they do. I think a great example of this is life on earth. I am constantly told by Archangel Gabriel that life is easy; we make it hard. I feel it's a similar idea when it comes to the universe. For example, we're told the universe is infinite. We may not fully be able to grasp what infinity looks like, but we understand the concept.)

I am, and I think that's really fascinating to see. Thanks for pointing that out. Can we go back to the lesson, though?

Gabriel: Yes, and know it is connected to Love and All. What I want to share with you is that the words *love* and *life* are interchangeable. Love can be channeled through your thoughts and ideas. You get this. I can tell. So the next thing I will say is that the time has come for the planet to understand this concept.

This goes back to things I've shared numerous times and even in the last lesson. You are a creator. You are creating your life moment by moment by moment. You create the love affair. You create yourself being poor or rich. You create yourself being happy or sad. *Create* is also another way of saying choose, or choice. You are *choosing* to be in a love affair. You are *choosing* to be poor. You are *choosing* to be happy or *choosing* to be sad. Happiness is a choice. Love is a choice. Financial wealth is a choice. Wealth in all other ways is also a choice. You are choosing all of it.

Beau, there is nothing big and secret to share with you at a certain point because it's all the same: Everything is a choice.

Things happen and then you have the free will to choose how to react to them. Love is everything.

What more would you like me to tell you? I can tell you about other planets and galaxies and what God is in greater detail, and that isn't going to serve you in any way. I am here to share with you and the world three things: (1) Everything is made from Love. It is a Love greater than you understand. (2) Everything is a choice. *Everything.* You are a creator. You are God in human form. What God isn't, is a physical being up in the sky ready to judge you. (3) God is energy. God is everything, for God is energy and everything is made of energy. This is what I mean by the Universe and everything about it is simple.

Well, all right! I guess there is nothing else to talk about or ask about with these lessons.

Gabriel: Take what I gave you and use it in your life. Watch magic happen. It always works when you apply it.

Thank you, Gabriel.

Hi, Gabriel. How are you doing today?

Gabriel: I am always great, Beau. How are you?

I'm really well. I have my friend coming over to help turn the office into my studio!

(I used to make a lot of music.)

Gabriel: Yay! So here we go. The next lesson I gave you is: *Power and strength lie in numbers.* This is not just the idea of people coming together, but also ideas full of power and strength. The more ideas of power and strength you have, the better to operate with.

This is a big deal and something I want you to get, Beau. The power of your thoughts is key to your survival. Life is all about momentum. Use those endless numbers of ideas of power and strength to *give* you power and strength. Then create a team and use that team as your physical power and strength. One without the other isn't as workable.

When it comes to a big project, you want to brainstorm everything first if you want to get the most out of it. For instance, use this opportunity moving the studio into the office and having your friend help as a chance to put this into action. Walk into the room and look at the best way to lay it out. After you do that, you can use your friend's help to apply the changes. It'll always work out in your favor.

Well, that's an interesting way to look at it. I will go and do that after this channeling and maybe even do it *with* my friend! Two people brainstorming are better than one, right?

Gabriel: You are getting this lesson so well. Keep at it. Go and see what you can do, and when your friend comes, look at other things you can create.

Thank you, Gabriel, for a great idea.

Gabriel: Always, Beau, in all ways. I am of service to you and the world.

Good morning, Gabriel. It's a beautiful day, wouldn't you say?

Gabriel: Always, it is a beautiful day. Remember, it is all about perception.

Yes, it is. So, I see that the next lesson you gave me is: *Each adolescent youth is burdened with the pleasure of life.* Can you please speak more about that?

Gabriel: Yes. Have you ever met a sad baby? How often do you meet sad children? I realize that in your country, it's not too often. We're talking about little kids and babies. In other countries, there are children who are hurting. I want you to get though that these things are taught. Sadness is taught. Depression is taught. Pain is taught. When a child is born, he's not sad; he's happy. This is a new spirit coming into the world, so he's happy. Society puts ideas into his subconscious that may make him sad.

It's a choice put on the child, just as it is as you get older. What you learn in childhood, you bring with you into your life as you get older. Some learn to stop it from running their lives, and others don't. Know that each child is burdened with the pleasure of life because that is all they know life to be at birth and through the first few years of their life. They are burdened with it because this is what they were given when they entered life.

(This is a reminder that all of the ways we are, as far as how we act and react in and to life, are started in our childhood.)

I definitely get that. Can you please explain this in more detail though? What more can you say on this subject?

Gabriel: You expect me to express to you different options about topics. Beau, there is nothing more to share for a lot of things. I'd just be wording them differently. What are you expecting me to say specifically that is going to make this topic more readable and exciting for you?

I think it's the fact that your presence isn't coming through as strong, and so I kind of feel like I'm making this up. I also realize this is due to my vocabulary and grammar.

(I would still question if this were really Archangel Gabriel coming through or if I were just making it all up. There are many times, especially during some of these channels, that I would only get so much information. Also, only words I know are used. I didn't really receive any new words.)

Gabriel: If you ever think that you have anything holding you back, you should stop that, for it does not serve you, Beau. *You are the only thing that is holding you back from anything.* It's that simple. Remember what you learned about that guy you just met? After studying self-development, he realized he could do anything and so he started building drones. He has no expertise in building mechanical objects. He is not a mechanical engineer. He's just a man with a way of making things happen and a knowing that he can *do anything.*

(I met this guy at a gathering to talk about what we'd accomplished from studying self-development work.)

So I ask you, Beau, what is holding you back from understanding this and understanding yourself and understanding that you can do anything? Once you can get past this, you can have everything you ever dreamed of. There is no coincidence with anything that happens to you, ever. You are creating everything, for there is nothing that is controlling your life but your thoughts. That's it. It's as simple as that. I am speaking to you the way I am speaking to you because this is how you talk. This is how you speak. If this came across so drastically different, then you wouldn't believe it even more so. Life is a series of actions and thoughts and ideas.

Beau, stop intellectualizing everything. Remember, you are doing this to yourself. You are living the life you are creating every millisecond of every moment.

Well, since you put it like that . . .

Gabriel: Let us move to the next lesson: *You control your destiny.* Only you. See how I brought this lesson in to work with what we just spoke about? The point I want to make here is that *you control all of your life.* What you see is then processed through the thoughts and ideas that you have about life. That is why there are separate political parties. That's why there are wars. That's why you are a nice person. That's why others are mean. That's why people are killed. That's why people are healed of pain and disease.

Destiny is created by the individual. Destiny is not something everyone is here to obtain, but know that regardless, you are still creating your life moment by moment. Remember, all there is . . . is Now. And Now. And Now. And Now. That's *it.* I'm not sure how much simpler this can be explained to people. "Now" is all that exists and all that has ever existed. *Now* backwards is *won.* You won! Isn't that great? Every moment of life you are winning. As long as you stay in the Now, you've won.

It really is *that* simple, isn't it?

Gabriel: Beau, once you realize this, life will be so much easier to understand and live through.

Thank you for constantly telling me this. It's obvious you are trying to make a point.

Gabriel: I am not *trying* to do *anything*. I am simply spreading my knowledge and love. However long it takes and how[ever] many times I have to share it.

Is that it for today?

Gabriel: Yes. Go about your day with this knowledge and see what happens. I'm excited!

Ha. So am I.

Hola, Gabriel! I am excited to channel you this morning!

Gabriel: I am excited you channeled me!

So I see the next lesson you shared with me is: *The devastations of your life are created by the circumstances of your effort.* That's a mouthful for what seems like something relatively simple to understand.

Gabriel: They *(the lessons)* come into your mind that way to let you know that *you* are not making it up. They're a little abstract to make sure they stick out. Also, you have an angel speaking through you. This is how I talk.

Obviously. So please explain more about this lesson.

Gabriel: Sure thing. The "devastations of your life" sounds worse than how I mean it, but bear with me. When I say *devastations,* I mean when things don't work out according to plan. So we can use the word *alternative.* When the alternatives for your life don't work out, it *(the result)* is created by the thoughts you are creating, which leads to the actions you are taking. It's really that simple.

This goes back to the last two lessons about how you are creating *everything.* There is no right or wrong here. It's a matter of you doing something that goes against what you had in mind originally, or bringing about something different than you expected to have happen and then [realizing that] the effort you put across is not what you wanted. Do you get this?

I'm still trying to figure out "the circumstances of my effort."

(Stay with this.)

Gabriel: This is easy. The circumstances of your effort are just that: circumstances. What is a circumstance? Simply put, it is what you are currently dealing with. So devastations in your life are different expectations happening. These are ones that you are no longer controlling (at least you think that, but let's carry on.) When those devastations happen, you are still in control. Now you can say that you have to deal with the current circumstances. Are you following?

(I've realized that many things come through based on how I interpret them, so let me clear this up. This sentence I received from Archangel Gabriel is saying that the way we think and the things we end up doing based on how we think attract things/situations to us. Those things/situations we attract cause our world, meaning our life, to look how it does. This all goes back to the Law of Attraction.)

I think so. Stuff happens—the circumstances. So the things happening in my life that aren't going terribly wrong based on my expectations are created by my effort. Circumstances are what I now have to deal with. My effort is my effort. I'm currently dealing with the circumstances of my effort. The stuff that's happening that isn't going according to plan is created by what I'm dealing with through my . . . actions?

Gabriel: Keep going, Beau. You're getting it.

So my thoughts and actions are creating my results. Life happens the way it happens, and at some level we are creating it subconsciously. When things happen, we have a choice how to respond to them. Am I getting anywhere with this? Because I feel like I'm missing a piece at the end.

Gabriel: All you are missing is belief in yourself, Beau. We also talked about this recently. Believe in yourself. Read the next lesson.

The channeling of life is manifested by the education of your thoughts. I feel like this is almost a simpler way to explain the last lesson. Am I right about that?

Gabriel: Yes. It is a simpler way of explaining it. You channel life how you see it. Your thoughts are creating all of it. Remember that you are God in human form. God created everything through thought. God has an infinite education and intelligence. You are God in human form. Once you really get that, you'll realize that you can do anything.

I think this is a great way to end today's channeling.

Gabriel: And so it is.

Thank you, Gabriel, for this gift. It's incredibly appreciated.

Gabriel: You deserve it.

Hello, Gabriel! What's up?

Gabriel: Same ol' same ol'. The only thing that has changed is *you.*

In what way? Mentally? Physically? Spiritually?

Gabriel: Let's just say you've grown in all three areas. Remember, don't take things to heart. Taking it to heart is a choice, and this understanding is something you could carry throughout the rest of your life.

That's true. I will do my best not to take things to heart, but I'm only human.

Gabriel: I'm glad that you understand that. Nothing and no one is perfect.

(Everything is a choice, first and foremost. I mean this in terms of how we react to things. Allow yourself to be human and make choices that may not be the best at the moment. We learn by trial and error.)

Correct. So it looks like the next lesson you gave me is: *Internal energies move throughout the mind.* Please explain this further, Gabriel.

Gabriel: Absolutely, I will. *Internal energies* refers to how you feel about yourself inside—the things *you* think are what occur in the physical plane. If you feel like you aren't worth what you'd like to be, then that will manifest into your physical reality. If you think you're great, that will also manifest into your physical reality. If you think a project you're working on will go wonderfully, then it will.

Remember, though, that life happens, and while you may expect it to work out wonderfully along the way, it may not. It is still a choice on your part whether it'll go according to plan when all is said and done. Remember, life happens on the road to success. Successful people keep moving along the course no matter what the obstacles look like. They look internally and figure out how to best handle the situation if it starts going off course. Those people who aren't successful blame everything for why they aren't successful. Do you understand this?

Yes, I do.

(To make this clearer, you may think something you're doing is going to go great. It may even go great at the beginning, and then something happens that stops it dead in its tracks. It may even completely fall apart, and you have to start all over. The point is: Life happens. We can expect the best and know in our heart it's going to work out, and then it doesn't for one reason or another. This is where making choices comes into play, which Archangel Gabriel keeps saying. Will we give up when things don't go according to plan, or will we rise up and try again? It's all a choice.)

Gabriel: OK, good. This goes back to everything we've ever talked about. You are God in human form. You are energy. Energy is everything, which means that energy is God. Once you can understand that everything is energy and everything is God, you'll realize that you are truly manifesting it all. Every single obstacle of life is channeled through thoughts. Thoughts can be called *feelings*. Your feelings about yourself, about your life, about situations, about everything are why your life goes the way it goes.

Don't judge other people or outside circumstances. You still have a choice in how things go. Have integrity. If things aren't going according to plan and you need more time, then communicate that to whomever is waiting on whatever it is they are waiting on. Deliver on it when you say you will. Be careful of your actions and your thoughts because they can paralyze you and leave you internally crippled. There are no mistakes in the universe. There are only your thoughts and the actions you take based on those thoughts. Be aware of your influence on your environment. Keep calm and carry on *(as the British say!)*.

One thing I've really noticed is that all of these things you share are so much easier said than done.

Gabriel: Know that they are only easier said than done because you say so. Life is easy, Beau. Deal with it the best you can, but deal with it regardless. Being able to speak up is huge to your success. Be you. Be your best you. Your best you knows what to do when things go awry.

(Stand in your power. Remember, you are a creator, and everything *is a choice.)*

I do believe that. Again, it is just easier said than done. It's so easy to get in our own way. How can we stop that?

Gabriel: First, I want you to know that you will almost always get in your own way, even if it's for a split second. You'll doubt yourself. You'll say to yourself, "What's the point?" "I'm not doing that." "I can't have what I want." That's all self-deprecating. Recognize your power. Remember, you are God in human form. God didn't have any fear creating life throughout the universe. Why should you be scared, if God wasn't and you are God in human form? That would be a contradiction. You created life. When you manifest things that scare you, ask yourself, why am I manifesting this? Now, it could very well be for you to grow and help you get *past* fear. Other times, it could be to help you grow as a human being. Don't expect something extraordinary if you don't feel extraordinary.

Beautifully said, Gabriel. Is there anything else?

Gabriel: No.

Is that all for today's lessons?

Gabriel: Yes.

For an energy with so much personality and so much to talk about, you're being very terse.

Gabriel: I know. Go rest, my child.

OK. Bye, Gabriel.

Gabriel: Bye, Beau.

Gabriel, I love you!

Gabriel: I love you, too Beau. Be aware that your life is in your hands.

I definitely get that. Actually, it just hit me even more than usual. Anyway, I see the next lesson you gave me is: *The pilgrimage of life is sentenced to structure.* I'm pretty sure I understand that. Do you mean that the journey through life is only made through some kind of a structure? I have to plan out life for it to happen? Since it's up to me, I choose what happens? Is this what you mean?

Gabriel: Yes, but not completely.

(Dang it! Well, at least I was close.)

I just looked up the definition of *pilgrimage,* and it is "a journey." I then looked up the meaning of *pilgrim,* and it said "a person who journeys to a sacred place for religious reasons." How can I be on a pilgrimage if I'm not religious?

Gabriel: Beau, do you remember what I told you in the life lessons book, that the spirit culture is religious in its own way?

I just did a search in the life lessons book, and I came across this: "There is so much you have to learn and grow to a state of being that in itself is religious in a way of spirit." There is a state of being you wanted me to learn, and grow to that, in itself, is religious in the way of spirit? That's interesting. Can you please explain that further?

Gabriel: OK. The lesson here is to know that time is out to work with you. There is so much for you to get. The point is that the voice within you is not you; the voice within you is God.

God guides you. This is such a spiritual experience for humans. Remember, you are spiritual beings having a physical experience. The journey begins with believing. Obviously, you don't have to believe in spirit to be on a journey. What I mean is, you have to believe in the journey. You have to believe you will get to where you want to get. There is a religious aspect to this, that you have to have absolute faith and trust in something you can't see. Do you get that?

That seemed to be a long explanation for that. Tell me more, though.

Gabriel: The journey is religious in the way of spirit. If you trust only yourself, then you are believing in God, for you are God in human form. *Even if you don't believe in yourself, you are still being guided.* You don't have to see it for it to be real. Remember that, for we will get back to that a little later in these lessons.

Religion as it is today is taken out of context when it comes to things people follow in books and stories. It's not that some of these stories didn't happen. They did. The biggest flaw is that people take them so out of context. Follow your heart and believe in it. It doesn't matter what really happened or not. If you fully believe in something, then honor it and live life through the lessons you've learned from that way of thinking. Don't take the word *religious* so seriously, Beau, for the word, in your personal world, has been tainted.

(*"You don't have to see it for it to be real"* is one of the most important things we have to learn, in my opinion. There is so much energy around us, but we can't see it. Spirits are around, but a lot of us can't see them. Just because we can't see them doesn't mean they don't exist.)

So then, please share a proper definition for the word *religious*.

Gabriel: Believing that all is the way it is, regardless of actual truth.

That almost seems insulting, "regardless of actual truth."

Gabriel: You create that meaning. "Insulting" is a choice.

Goodness, Gabriel. That whole "X is a choice" is getting a little old. It almost seems like an excuse, a way not to take any responsibility for your actions.

Gabriel: I know. You're making all that up, though. There is nothing "wrong" with what I said. The way you are taking it is a personal view.

(Everything *is a choice. This is also a huge lesson for us to learn.*)

You are making a great point, but I don't want to deal with it. Well played, Gabriel. Is there anything else you'd like to share regarding this lesson or any other lessons you'd like to share with me during this channeling?

Gabriel: No. I will share more tomorrow.

Till next time, then.

Good morning, Gabriel. How are you?

Gabriel: If I told you how excited I was to be here with you, you wouldn't believe me.

Why not?

Gabriel: You've personally never reached *this* level of excitement!

Can I reach that level of excitement as a human being?

Gabriel: Yes, you can. That's all you need to know.

So regarding the next lesson, I remember wondering if it was actually a lesson or something that came to me at the moment just as a quick reminder. It is: *You can do this on your own. Everything happens for a reason. Shhh. Be quiet and listen.* It is definitely legit. I just didn't know if it was meant to be a lesson for me to ask more about.

Gabriel: Does it matter if it was? Let's discuss that. There are people out there who don't think they can do things on their own. They think they need "help." This is not true. That's not to say that getting help is detrimental to their growth. What it means is that people out there don't have enough confidence in themselves to do things alone. They don't trust themselves. That's what this lesson comes down to. This is where the "be quiet and listen" comes into effect. If you don't think you can do it, if you don't think you know what to do, then silence your mind and listen within. Listen to us guide you. It always works; when you listen to us, it always works out in your favor. You have to listen, though. Block out all internal dialogue to reveal what is really there for you. The truth will be told to you. The best plans of action will be told to you if you trust in yourself.

(When you can tell the difference between your own thoughts and guidance from the angels, blocking out internal dialogue that you create yourself will be so much easier.)

So the basic message is to trust in ourselves.

Gabriel: You got it.

I was going to say that is so much easier said than done, but we just talked about that. Sometimes, we just have to do it.

Gabriel: Just do it—as Nike says. You laugh, but it is true. They released a great message to the world: "Just do it." Even if you don't trust yourself, just do it. This is so simple, and yet people fight it. Life would go so much smoother for a lot of people if they just did what they had to do instead of fighting it. Things would get done much quicker. Trust in yourself and just do it.

I believe that. Lord knows I've held off on things. We all do it.

(I've procrastinated so much over my life. I can't believe I just shared that.)

Gabriel: Not everyone. Most, but not everyone. The most successful people get things done at the moment they have to be done. Also, realize that even they hold off on certain things, and it's usually to get other things done that they decide are more important. That's a choice. What is more important to you is a decision.

There is nothing wrong here. I just want you to know this.

Thank you. Is there anything else you'd like to share regarding this lesson?

Gabriel: No. We shall communicate more tomorrow.

OK. Bye, Gabriel.

Hello, Gabriel. Good morning.

Gabriel: Hi, Beau. Good morning to you. I am sure you are well, for I know so much about you.

I'm good. This next lesson I have here from you sounds so strange: *The paradigm of life is shifted by the curvature of safe.* Was there supposed to be a word after *safe,* or is that right how it is?

Gabriel: There is no mistake. Let me explain this in further detail. The way you look at life is shifted by what you consider safe and what you don't. Remember, it is all perception. The life you live is dedicated to the server of the mind, as we spoke about earlier. You are the server of your own mind. You serve it different variations of love and life. Be one with God during this matter. The paradigm of life is in regard to how you see life. It is shifted by what you consider safe. That's a simpler way to put it.

Now, "safe," as I said, is a perception. What is safe to you may not be safe to someone else. Your life is therefore viewed differently from someone else looking at your life and comparing it to their life and what *they* think is safe. Once you realize that everyone has a different view of life, you will understand how different everyone is.

That said, you are all the same. You are all One. The key here is to realize that each individual human is different in how they look at the world but the same at their core. "The paradigm of life is shifted by the curvature of safe" relates to how you view the world. This is different from my saying, "Your views and ways of being are different from theirs. Yours are better." I would never say that, and it is not so. You are all different, and yet you are all the same. Watch the news and see what I mean. While it is filled with anger and propaganda, it is filled with different views on the world. You will agree with some stories and disagree with others. Such is life as a human.

(We are all the same because we're all made of the same stuff, and we are all created by the same energy. We are all different because we're all unique. Then there is the idea of perception, *which is how we look at the world. We each look at it differently. This goes back to each of us being unique.)*

Couldn't you have just said "You're all different regarding how you view and think about the world, but you're still all the same because you are all One?" Wouldn't that have been much easier and far less wordy?

Gabriel: No, because there are many things that would not have been made clear. Trust my words, Beau. Always, in all ways.

Well, all right. Is there anything else you'd like to share?

Gabriel: No. This is all for today.

Gabriel! How are you doing today?

Gabriel: Beau, I am lovely as always.

I really didn't expect anything less. Let's get right to the next lesson you gave me, which is: *The characteristics of Life are determined by the characteristics of self.* Please speak more on this lesson, Gabriel.

Gabriel: Have I told you lately how much I love you? There is a reason I shared this sentence with you. The secret to life doesn't exist, but if there were one, it would be this: You get to choose your life. You get to choose how you live your life. You get to choose who to be regardless of what you look like or your upbringing, your circumstances, your skin color, your family history, etc. There are so many excuses that can be made to keep you at the small amount of power that you think you have. Leave the negative talk alone and carry on to be powerful. There are many reasons why you can't be powerful. Choose differently. Your circumstances do *not* define who you are or what you can do. Live, love, and laugh.

(Stand in your power. Always.)

Not for nothing, Gabriel, but I feel like there are things that are easier for me because of my current circumstances that may be harder for other people.

Gabriel: Take into consideration that some of the most successful people who have ever lived came from poverty; they found a way. If it's important enough, you will find a reason. If it's not, you will find an excuse. Don't hide. Don't shy away from power. Some people don't know anything different from their situation. They are given clues that they *can* be powerful and don't have to surrender to their circumstances. The worst thing a person can do to themselves is give up on themselves. Life is about choice. The end.

In other words, circumstances are just that—circumstances. They don't define who we are, though, or what we can do. I wish people could really get this. The motivational speaker Nick Vujicic has no limbs, but he didn't let that stop him from being powerful and empowering others. That's awesome. Is there anything else you'd like to share?

Gabriel: Be great. Be powerful. Be fruitful. Be courageous.

I will. Thank you, Gabriel.

Gabriel: Know your power. You are God in human form.

Indeed, we are. Bye, Gabriel!

(We create every single thing in our lives by choice, whether consciously or subconsciously. Like Archangel Gabriel said, it doesn't matter what we look like or where we came from. Life comes down to choices. Things happen, and then we decide how to handle them, whether we're aware of why we made that decision or not. It's really incredible to realize how amazing and powerful we actually are.)

Hi, Gabriel. I took a look at the list of lessons I've gotten from you and saw I only have three left. Should I expect more?

Gabriel: Listen and you will find I have an infinite number of lessons left to share with you.

Infinite?! You're telling me that the lessons never end?

Gabriel: Does learning ever end? Do you get to a point in your life when you say, "Looks like I've learned everything. Time to stop living!"?

Well, no, obviously not. Plus, I was just considering how the universe is infinite. That would have to mean that there is an infinite number of life lessons to be learned.

Gabriel: You are correct. You never stop learning. Even as a soul you learn. You are immortal. You learn forever. I am here to learn with you, and God learns through you.

You, Archangel Gabriel, learn *with* me? You're a messenger of God. You are far more intelligent than I am, so I would think you know *much* more about life than I do.

Gabriel: There is nothing like a good review.

Well said. Let's move on to the next lesson, which is: *Obligation is a choice.* While I know what an obligation is, I wanted to see what the actual definition was. According to the dictionary, it is "an act or course of action to which a person is morally or legally bound; a duty or commitment." So while I understand that everything is a choice, if you are legally bound to do something, I would think you'd *have* to do it.

Gabriel: And this brings up a great point. Choice is a decision. It's as simple as that. What I want to say is that with every choice, there is a consequence. The consequences of life are another way to teach you. For every action, there is an equal and opposite reaction; this is a law of the universe. There is a consequence for *whatever* you do. *Consequence* is not a bad word. It's just a word. You are making it mean something bad. The laws of life aren't "good" or "bad." They are just laws. Choose wisely and choose to have the best outcome work for you.

(To clarify, a choice is usually an unconscious decision. A decision is a conscious choice. One has a greater awareness in making a decision.)

That's hard to say when I see so much racism happening. An African-American man, as innocent as can be, gets treated differently in certain situations than a white man. It's just that simple. How can we have the best outcome work for us when I see viral racist videos pop up on the Internet showing an innocent African-American man standing on the corner doing *nothing* and getting harassed by a cop just because he's black? You teach me lessons like this, and all I can think about is how much easier this stuff is for someone like me in my position. There is so much negativity and violence and racism in this world.

Gabriel: Look at it like this: We are all here to be One with each other. I understand that decisions happen and racism happens and hate happens. You're only human; your ego gets in the way of love. It stops you from being One. Things happen that make people question whether or not there is a God. God is real, but let me get back to this point.

You have no obligation as a human being to be "nice" and "kind" to people. You have no obligation to love. You have no obligation to believe in God or me or anything you cannot see. People even *see* stuff and still don't believe it. There are no obligations to be anything. There is only choice. That's it. If you ever think that I am here to tell you to be a certain way, then you are wrong. That's not bad. That's just how it is.

Wow. I didn't see that one coming. That was a great way to teach me this lesson. With that said, I have to go. Thank you, Gabriel. Is there anything else you'd like to share about this lesson before I go?

Gabriel: There is nothing. Take care, Beau.

I always get a big smile on my face when you enter! Why is that?

Gabriel: What else would you expect to happen? I am pure love energy transmitted through your being. Of course you're going to smile!

Awesome. OK, so the lesson you gave me recently was: *Travel the road less traveled.* That seems easy enough to understand, but I would still love a more in-depth explanation. What can you share about this lesson, Gabriel?

Gabriel: If I told you how powerful you are, I would blow your socks off. Let's get right to it. Traveling the road less traveled is a decision you have to make, for it is not for everyone when it comes to how well a person can handle the stress. It comes with a lot of ups and downs, and you have to be willing to take on that challenge. Are you ready to take on that challenge?

See, it doesn't matter what you are trying to accomplish, but you should know at the end of that less-traveled road is always success. Even when things seem tough and look like they are never going to get better, look inside for the right answer. Use your intuition as a GPS and let it guide you to the right destination. Capacity of Self is measured by the commitment of passion. Process in the integrity of Self and let it be measured by the breaths you take. Learn to be One with God and follow your heart, for your heart is the greatest GPS ever invented. Follow your instincts, for your heart and your instincts are interconnected. Follow your soul because it already knows the best route to take. It has laid out the map for you.

This doesn't mean that your life is predestined. It just means your soul has created other ways for you to follow since you have the ability to have free will. Remember, life is a choice. Only you are the willing participant in your life's creation. Everything else will manifest based on how you think.

(To be clear, free will can offer you multiple paths, as you choose.)

In other words, if we get lost on our way to our goal, stop, take a deep breath, and look inside for the answer as to what to do next?

Gabriel: Basically, yes. Go for the gold, always, in all ways. You are your only adversary. No one else matters when it comes to competition. It is about you and you only. Always do your best to outdo yourself, to be better than who you were. It's fun. Don't beat yourself up if you can't reach the goal of doing "better" than last time. Take what you've learned and apply it to the next venture.

This lesson is so simple and a wonderful reminder to be the best you can be always, in all ways. Is there anything else you'd like to share regarding this lesson?

Gabriel: There is nothing else. I have shared it all with you. Remember, life is a choice. If you decide not to follow your instincts, that is a decision and that is fine. You will *never ever* be judged, for God does not judge. Think about this: How do you feel when you judge yourself? How do you feel when others judge you? Most people don't feel that great. So if you are God in human form, why would God ever judge Itself if It has learned from you that it stinks to judge yourself or have others judge you? That doesn't make anybody accomplish happiness.

God has learned from *us* about judgment?

Gabriel: God understands the concept of judgment. God learns through you; therefore, God experiences judgment of self at every moment. It's a terrible feeling to put upon yourself. God loves you *infinitely*. Why would God ever put you in harm's way?

If God never judges, then that makes sense. If you love something or someone unconditionally, you wouldn't want to have them/it be hurt. At least, that's how I see it. Others may think differently. I think some people put the one they love in harm's way intentionally to teach that person a lesson.

Gabriel: That does happen. However, this isn't God's way of doing things. This goes back to the life lesson in the first book about God never pulling a practical joke on you. Practical jokes can scare and hurt people. Why would God ever want to scare or hurt you? God is love. God *only* loves you. That's it. Anyone who thinks that God is judgmental or hurts people or things on purpose is incorrect.

I would agree with that wholeheartedly. Is there anything else you'd like to share?

Gabriel: That is all, and I am proud of you for channeling me every day.

Thank you. Take care, Gabriel!

Good morning, Gabriel. How are you?

Gabriel: Beau, I am beautifully accepted by God.

I've never heard that one before. Wow.

Gabriel: Know that you all are accepted beautifully by God.

I will take that into consideration. I don't really know what else to say. Let's move on to the last lesson I have from you: *Energy devotes itself to love.* Please explain more about this, Gabriel.

Gabriel: Time to learn about this lesson. Know that we are all One. The time has come for you to know that the concept of life is almost exactly what you think it is, based on all of the lessons I have shared with you. Human beings are souls at their core. Souls are spirit at their core. Spirit is energy at its core. Energy is love at its core. Therefore, energy devotes itself to itself. It takes on a slightly different form. It takes on the form of love.

Love is all there is, Beau. Do you get that? *Love is all there is,* and it is a love that a human being, a soul, and a spirit will never fully understand. The amount of love God has for each and every one of you and each and every living and nonliving thing is not measurable in human thought. It is a love beyond your understanding. You have to realize that there are things out there that the human brain just can't conceptualize. That's fine, and that doesn't make you stupid. You are all geniuses.

If we are all geniuses, then why can't we fully grasp that?

Gabriel: Because a) geniuses don't know *everything,* and b) you are not supposed to understand that.

That stinks. I want to know.

> **Gabriel:** Beau, if I told you about the love of God and shared that love with you, it would overwhelm you. The closest idea I can give you is how much your mom loves you—and you'll experience that same kind of love when you have children. Know that the time will come when you get the idea of pure love when you become a parent. You are starting to conceptualize it with your niece.

All right, I have to accept that. What else would you like to share about this lesson?

> **Gabriel:** I'll tell you this: The movement of energy that surrounds you is immeasurable. All you need to know is that you are made of love and nothing more. Everything will come full circle in the end. I promise you this.

(We are pure love. It's not a romantic love. This is universal love. God's love. It is a love we can't even fully grasp.)

OK. Is there anything else?

> **Gabriel:** There is nothing else.

All right, then. Take care, Gabriel, and thank you.

> **Gabriel:** Be kind, peaceful, and loving.

Hi, Gabriel. It's practically afternoon. How are you?

Gabriel: I am always doing well. How are you?

I am great. I just worked out and had a *super*-healthy after-workout shake. I feel fit and healthy.

Gabriel: Excellent. Keep doing that. It's great for you. So let us get to the next lesson since we have gone through all the ones I gave you. The lesson is: *Be self-sufficient. Be reliable. Have integrity with others and with yourself.* People forget how important integrity is with themselves. People give, give, and give to others and then never give to themselves, *or* they give, give, and give to themselves but never to others. Find a balance.

(One of the biggest lessons I've learned over the past two years is how import-ant balance is. This is not physical balance. It's meant not to go overboard with certain tasks or ways of being. It's meant as keeping everything equal. Balance in our lives helps us stay grounded and avoid being scatterbrained. Imagine a life where we give a healthy amount of time to everything.)

I agree that a lot of people do that. What does giving to others have to do with being self-sufficient though?

Gabriel: The key here is to have integrity with everything you do. This brings us to another lesson, which is to be aware of how you want karma to come back to you. People forget that doing things that will hurt others, even though they bring money or hap-piness, will cause karma to come and smack them in the back of the head when they least expect it. Be kind to others. The karma that comes back from being loving is so much more wonderful to have happen to you than something you consider bad.

Be aware that life is up to you. It is your choice to live how you want. I am suggesting that to make your life easier, you be kind to others and be kind to yourself. Treat yourself and others like a temple. Pay attention when there is misconduct in that temple. Adjust your actions if need be.

(God/Universe is not judgmental at all. However, there is karma, and it is simply brought on by you. This is a great reminder to stay kind as often as you can, not just to others but to yourself. Remember, being kind is a choice.)

That's powerful, Gabriel. That's like the lesson I've heard throughout my life: *Treat your body like a temple.*

Gabriel: Where do you think it came from? God is assisting everyone and everything at all times, always, in all ways. Clues to live the best life are delivered from time to time to help you be your best.

(I definitely consider this book a clue. Do you?)

That's so powerful. Is there anything else you'd like to share with me regarding either of those lessons?

Gabriel: The key ingredient to all of this is to be Love. Be ambitious. Be self-sufficient. Assist when you need to and learn to take care of yourself so when you help others, it is from a place of experience.

That's awesome. Thank you for sharing. Is there anything else?

Gabriel: If you would like more, I will share, but as far as these lessons go for today, there is no more to share about them.

OK. We will move on tomorrow. Thank you, Gabriel, for this gift. I am touched.

Hi, Gabriel. Good morning to you. As soon as I sat down to start channeling, the sentence "Clandestine opportunities appear to those who wait" came to me. I imagine that is the life lesson you'd like to share today? *Clandestine* means "secret." Why would secret opportunities appear to those who wait?

Gabriel: Have you ever thought about how I am using the word *secret?* Don't look at it as a bad thing. Let me clear this up. The word *secret* is used in the sense that the average person (most people, in this particular case) isn't going to think about the particular action that is manifesting in her mind. It is a "secret" because no one ever knew or thought about this opportunity. It is a secret because the spirit world never really inspired many people with this particular challenge.

Take the word *secret* as a missed opportunity that is inspired. The spirit world wants people to be their best and do their best. There's nothing like sharing a message with someone on how to do something that is different from anybody else, for that is the thing that allows people to manifest their dreams differently from the usual way. Don't ever disregard a message that sounds crazy, because it will usually work. It may be out of the ordinary, but don't write it off. If you only knew how often these opportunities are passed up and how often they work when they aren't [overlooked].

Don't ever completely get rid of an inspired thought. Writing off these messages will slow down what you're trying to accomplish. It's easy. Life is easy. The ego doesn't want you to grow. It wants to keep you small, for that is the job of the ego. The ego does its job to keep you safe, but sometimes you have to take risks to accomplish your dreams and goals. Such is life, Beau. Such is life.

(Don't pass up great ideas that appear in your mind. Always find a way to accomplish them no matter how impossible they seem. I remember hearing many years ago that an idea or skill/ability will be passed off to someone else if you don't do it. I don't know about you, but that kind of scares me because I want to be the one who does it first. It is given to you because you can do it. Don't ever doubt that.)

This is a really cool lesson, Gabriel. So, we should listen to inspired thought even if it sounds totally nuts, because if we do things based on those inspired thoughts instead of writing them off, we will accomplish our goal. Did I explain that right?

Gabriel: Listen to your instincts. That's just another way of saying "Listen to your inspired thoughts." Trust your instincts always because they are right every single time. Your instincts are the key that unlocks opportunity.

(It's moments like these that remind me this isn't me talking. That last line is breathtaking.)

That's brilliant, Gabriel. I'm inspired!

Gabriel: Don't mix up your inspired thoughts with your ego. Your ego will steer you in the wrong direction at times. That's what it's there for. Your ego doesn't want you to win. It wants to win.

Are you saying that the ego's purpose is to sabotage you?

Gabriel: Not completely, but it will if you listen to it over your instincts. Remember, trust your first thought when it comes to instincts. Your first thought is the right thought because your first thought is usually based on feeling. That's instinct. If you're standing at the edge of a cliff, and it's not a far fall but you're scared, the ego will keep you in fear and won't want you to jump. If your instincts are telling you, "You will be OK. You can jump. Jump to the left. It's safer than jumping to the right," then *trust that.* Trust in your instincts, Beau. Always, in all ways, trust your instincts.

(That is based on pure trust of your instincts. I'd like to add that your ego does keep you safe, but there are moments when staying safe isn't always for your best and highest good.)

I will. Is there anything else you'd like to share about these lessons?

Gabriel: No. That is all for these lessons.

All right, I have to go get ready. Thank you so much, Gabriel, for sharing this. It is beautiful.

Gabriel: Keep at it. I like the fact I am talking to you every morning.

I like it, too.

Hi, Gabriel. I always crack up when you enter for a channeling. It's my sign to let me know you are there. I love it so much.

Gabriel: I know, and I enjoy you channeling me. We can talk about this all day. Let's get to the next lesson I'd like to share with you. This life lesson is: *Be prepared for the worst, and expect the best.*

Don't *expect* the worst. Just prepare for it in case it shows up, so you're ready if it does. Always expect the best outcome, though?

Gabriel: You got it, dude! *(As the Olsen Twins used to say on* Full House!*)* You are right. Always *prepare* for the worst possible outcome since you never know what life will throw at you. Be expecting the best possible outcome, though.

Here is an example. Imagine you are getting ready for the King's Ball. You are the princess, and you are dressed to perfection, head to toe. You think to yourself, *I look flawless,* and everyone else says the same thing. As you are walking down the stairs, your left heel on your high heels breaks, and you almost fall. You don't have a backup heel. That was your only one. Now what?

If you had prepared for the worst, you'd have a backup and could laugh it off. It'd make you and everyone else feel good. Laughter is the best medicine. If only you had remembered that other high heel, life would be much easier.

Or would it? Here is where the plot/story gets interesting. Your heel breaks and you didn't prepare for the worst. Now what? Well, two things could happen from here: You could either be sad and miserable about your heel, or you could kick *both* your high heels off, walk down the stairs barefoot, and go through the rest of the night like that.

Don't let the "worst" affect you when it happens, especially if you didn't prepare for it. Work with what you have. Throw your hands up and party. Remember, happiness is a choice. It is up to you how you handle an uncomfortable situation. Keep calm and carry on, as is said by the British. Be present always.

That's awesome. I love that. In other words, be your best at all times, even when the situation can knock you down.

Gabriel: Correct. Remember, everything happens for a reason. It is your choice, however, to choose how you will respond.

(Kick up your heels and party! That sounds like fun! Remember, don't take life too seriously. Enjoy it as much as you possibly can, and laugh things off as often as you can.)

I love it. Is there anything else you'd like to share, or is that the end of this lesson?

Gabriel: That is the end of this lesson, and we will keep on moving tomorrow. Good job.

Thank you. Take care, Gabriel.

Good morning, Gabriel. How are you?

Gabriel: I am always better than the day before.

Well, isn't that great to hear? Anyway, what would you like to share with me this morning? Is it a new lesson, or something else about the universe, or something completely different from those two things?

Gabriel: Conceptualize nothing, for nothing is every single object ever invented on this planet for God. The Creator is out to manifest love and beauty through everything and nothing at the same time. The concept of life is hard to grasp at times for human beings. Believe in nothing and believe everything. Be curious. Be logical (use common sense) and act with favor toward everything that walks this earth.

I don't even know how that makes any sense. Please clarify, Gabriel.

Gabriel: I want you to listen to everything I'm saying. The curiosity of the world depends on the cyclical energies of the soul, mind, and body. The ostentatious outcome of life is determined all in all by God. The life that you understand is different from the life that is actually going on at this moment. There are two things to realize, Beau: a) There is only love on this planet and b) There is only love that is broadcast throughout the stars. Serendipity is forthcoming.

(What I feel is meant by this is that our curiosity as a human race depends on our thoughts and actions. How God/the Universe displays life to us is simply how things are. If we are God/the Universe in human form, then life shows up as how we see it. This goes back to choice. It is our choice how we see things. We see life how we choose to see it instead of what's actually

happening. All that said, God/the Universe is love, and love moves through us, every single thing on the planet, the planet itself, space, the other planets, and the stars.)

I have to say that this is one of those conversations that are hard to believe only because your messages aren't coming in as clearly as usual. I feel like I'm making a lot of this stuff up.

> **Gabriel:** You're overthinking. Don't do that, for it slows you down and absolutely makes you want to question everything. Write down what I say for now, and you can review it afterwards. It always makes sense to you when you do that, especially when it is read back to you by someone else. Be aware that, as it always has been with us, my communication may not always be clear upon first hearing. Most of the time it is, and sometimes it is not. That's OK. Believe in what I share with you. That is all I am asking for.

I will, considering that even if I didn't believe everything else I've channeled, it was definitely you. There is a difference between how you speak and how I speak.

> **Gabriel:** Now you have the right attitude. Believe me. You don't *have* to, but I would highly impress upon you to do so.

Now that we have that out of the way, is there anything else you'd like to share regarding this lesson?

> **Gabriel:** No. Review this lesson when you can, and it will make sense to you.

I will. Thank you, Gabriel.

> **Gabriel:** Always.

AUGUST 29, 2014 • 9:07 A.M.

Hi, Gabriel. What lesson can you share with me today?

Gabriel: *The cherished soul is omniscient to the world around it.*

(I believe Gabriel means that the soul already knows everything when it comes here to Earth.)

So the cherished soul knows of everything in the world around it? I had to look up the definition to get clear on the word *omniscient*. I knew the word but was never clear on the meaning. The dictionary defined *omniscient* as God, probably because the word means "all knowing." *The cherished soul is God to the world around it.* Please explain this in more detail.

Gabriel: The deity of life is here to let you know that everything is One. God, you, the trees, the whole forest, outer space, and everything about outer space is God. It is omniscient. The *cherished soul* relates to *every* soul of *every* being. Every single soul ever of all of time is cherished. Therefore, every soul is aware of the world around it. It is One with the world around it. This goes back to what I've always told you. The presence of greatness lies within you and around you. Everything is greatness. Everything is One. Everything is God. God is One. You are God. You are One with God.

(God/the Universe is everything. Everything is God/the Universe. We are God/the Universe in human form. Archangel Gabriel's words may sometimes not make sense, but it all goes back to one of the biggest lessons, that we are all One. We are all connected.)

I love it. What else can be said?

Gabriel: That is the point. There is nothing else to say. Let's move on to another lesson.

You had me start typing a new lesson, and I couldn't believe what I was typing so I stopped. Let's try that again. What is this next lesson you'd like to teach me, Gabriel?

Gabriel: You have to let me finish, silly goose. *Compromise will lead to failure if not followed by integrity on your part and on the other party's part* (if there is another party involved). See, learn to work with others. Learn to do the best you can do and then do better. Go above and beyond. Beyond the cosmos of compromise lies the success of a generation that is hidden from its own sight. The slightest slip on your part can lead to a lack of integrity on a project, and you don't want that.

You want always to put out your best work. Sometimes, that is possible. Sometimes, it is not possible, but only in your head. I say "sometimes" because I want you to get that the earth rotates due to the flux of the universe. It is perfect. The universe only knows how to do its best. The world is on a tilt because that's how it works the best. You may think, why in the world is the world tilted? Easy: It functions best at the tilt it is on. Any slight shift will have things not work as smoothly. Sometimes, the least likely shift and change you expect to work is the best possible outcome.

(What I feel Archangel Gabriel means by all of this is to keep integrity with everything you do. In other words, stick to your word and always do the right thing. When you compromise with another party, do what you said you'd do and go above and beyond that. Remember always to do the right thing. The Universe always does what it has to do. It always keeps its word. If we are God/the Universe in human form and it has integrity, then we should, too.)

I almost feel like this is related to something my mom says all the time: "The harder you work, the luckier you get." Is that right?

Gabriel: Not really, but I see your point. Be One with God at the moment you begin new ideas and projects and have to work with others to set standards.

In other words, be your best. Be the best you?

Gabriel: That is much better. You are exactly right.

OK, good! I'm glad I understood that.

Gabriel: There is something missing, though, in all of this, which I haven't shared yet. That missing piece is not to let compromise make you not put forth your own ideas. Just because you have to compromise doesn't mean you have to follow it all. Only go with what is truly in your gut to do. Don't go overboard with it, though. A little extra won't hurt, because when you do things small with your best effort, sometimes that makes the biggest impact.

This is not about cheating or being hardheaded or doing things incorrectly and breaking the rules. Be yourself and do your best. I would never tell you to cheat. I would never say anything that would cause you to get in trouble or do wrong or make someone else upset, angry, or hurt.

(I feel Archangel Gabriel is simply saying to stand your ground and do the right thing. Regardless of how the compromise looks, you can still do your absolute best. This is where integrity comes into play.)

That's *almost* how it came across. I see your point though. Is there anything else?

Gabriel: Be aware that the Omniscient is all knowing. The All Knowing always has your back and always wants you to put your best foot forward. Be your best. Be fair. Be of integrity with yourself and others. Always. I ove all, for love is all there is.

I love you, Gabriel. Thank you so much for all of this.

Gabriel: You are welcome. Be God!

Hi, Gabriel. Let's move on to another life lesson. What can you share with me today?

Gabriel: Learn to be in control.

What? Learn to be in control? I thought . . .

Gabriel: Do you see what I did there? You just "accidently" closed this document, worried if it saved before it closed. I'm not saying to be what you would call a control freak and control every single situation you are in. People would find that annoying more often than not. When I tell you to learn to be in control, it is in reference to how you control your life. What you do daily and at every moment. In other words, don't let other people control your thoughts or feelings or how you live your life. Be you, and be the best you can be at all times.

(This is just another reminder to stay in integrity with yourself and your life. I've learned that things work out better and easier when you're in integrity on a regular basis.)

So, be in control of your life, thoughts, and feelings. But that doesn't mean be a control freak. I get that. That's an interesting lesson when it comes to how it's worded. Gabriel, I'm hungry. I have to go eat something.

Gabriel: Be in control! Yay!

You're crazy, but I love you.

Good morning, Gabriel. In my mind, when I pictured you coming down from the sky and into my thoughts as I always do, you were holding a sheep and told me to look up the meaning of a sheep. It represents docility and conformity. I heard you say, "You lack creativity, individuality, and initiative to venture out on your own. You tend to go along with the group." Why are you showing me this, Gabriel?

Gabriel: To let you know that it is time to venture out on your own. You've been afraid to do things by yourself. You always ask for help and guidance. Trust your instincts. Learn along the way. That is what life is all about. Growth. Trust.

Does this have anything to do with today's lesson?

Gabriel: *Don't conform, ever.*

Is that today's lesson?

Gabriel: Yes, it is. This goes back to *be yourself.* Don't let others tell you how to be. Don't mold yourself in the same form as everyone else and play it safe. Take risks. Venture out on your own. Choose the way of the wise, and self-esteem will enter into your life.

In other words, don't follow the crowd. Be ourselves, and the right people will enter into our lives when we do?

Gabriel: You got it. That was easy, wasn't it?

(I know how hard it can be to be yourself. There is so much judgment from people, and it can be tough when it comes from the ones you love. Follow your own path. When you stop letting what other people think control you, you are free.)

Yes, it was. Is there anything else you'd like to share about that lesson?

> **Gabriel:** No, there is not, so let's go to the next lesson: *Cherish the moments of life where things just don't seem to be going "right."* The coming of love [in these situations] is meant to give a rise of power for your soul. The compromise you have to make for love to enter is to give up the hatred you have for whatever you hate at that moment.

So when things aren't going right and we are angry and upset, we should give that up to make room for love? By having love at that moment, the best outcome will emerge?

> **Gabriel:** You are super close. What I mean by this is that you are the one making the decision. You see, the situation can still not work out as you planned, and things can go "wrong," but know that how you react to them is where the gift of love really comes into play. You can take the worst situation and make it work in your favor. Don't ever doubt the authenticity that lies in your heart and the ambidextrous alternatives to life you have in your mind.

Ambidextrous alternatives? That is a mouthful! Can you explain that term in clearer detail?

> **Gabriel:** You possess multiple ways of being in your soul. You know how to make things happen and choose different options. You just don't give yourself credit for it. Anyway, you can take any situation that doesn't look like it's working in your favor and make it work for you. Don't ever doubt your creativity.

That's really great to be told. Are you trying to remind us that we are more powerful than we think?

> **Gabriel:** That is what I am *always* pointing out to you. Are you listening?

(Apparently, I'm not listening. Archangel Gabriel repeatedly saying that we are more powerful than we think is definitely something Gabriel wants us as a human race to realize. When we stand in our power, we are unstoppable.)

Not always. Maybe I am listening, but I'm not taking action around what you're saying.

Gabriel: Don't ever doubt your ability to soar. Be one with the eagles.

We should soar.

Gabriel: Take into consideration that you already do, Beau. Once human beings realize how *incredible* they actually are, the world will cease to exist the way they see it and a new dawn will emerge from the truth.

(That's incredible! Imagine what our civilization would look like in twenty years if we started today. How exciting!)

That is so cool! In other words, we are holding ourselves back from growing as a society into the best we can be?

Gabriel: You are getting it. Now go out and defeat the world you see to bring the new one in! By *defeat*, I don't mean harm. By *defeat*, I mean to bring a new light. Get rid of the old ways you are and let the new ones full of love emerge. Remember that life lesson I shared with you, that you are a butterfly?

("You are a butterfly," is a lesson from Archangel Gabriel in my previous book, Gabriel's Guidance.*)*

I do remember that. Is that everything you'd like to share?

Gabriel: Yes. Tune in tomorrow for more lessons!

Tune in? Lovely.

Good evening, Gabriel. What is today's life lesson?

Gabriel: Today's life lesson is tomorrow's education. The life lesson I'd like to teach you today is *to be responsible at all costs, always, as long as you live.*

("Today's life lesson is tomorrow's education." Wow! This is so profound. That's saying that the life lesson we read today will be learned as early as the next day. It almost sounds like we'd have an "Aha!" moment. These lessons are education for our life.)

I feel like we talked about this in a recent lesson. This is very similar to 100 percent responsibility. What is the difference between that lesson and this one?

Gabriel: There isn't much difference. If there is any slight difference, it is just to be clearer.

Be clearer about responsibility? In other words, take responsibility and take that responsibility no matter what, at all times? Is that what you mean?

Gabriel: Keep going.

Take 100 percent responsibility at all times, even when you don't want to? That's what a parent does, especially a single parent. At least, that's what I imagine since I'm not a parent myself.

(My love and respect goes out to all single parents.)

Gabriel: Think of life as a parent. You will do *anything* to make that child happy. Do *anything* to make *your* life happy. Do *anything* to make your life the best it can be. Be 100 percent responsible for your life, for *you* are the creator of it and nothing else.

Which means that we are God in human form.

Gabriel: God is *you* in spirit form.

That's deep. I've never read it like that. My understanding is that the spirit wants to move forward and grow. The soul wants comfort. I guess that's why as humans, we come here with our soul. Am I correct in this observation, Gabriel?

Gabriel: If the majority of you knew how unbelievable you are, it would blow your mind.

So you've told me. What else can you share about this lesson?

Gabriel: There is nothing else.

Is that it for tonight, then?

Gabriel: Yes. Channel me tomorrow morning, please.

I will. Thank you, Gabriel.

Gabriel: Be kind. Be peace and be love.

Hello, Gabriel. I made sure to channel you this morning, and it's actually been a little less than twelve hours. I'm happy about that.

Gabriel: So am I. Let's get right to it. The next lesson I want to teach you is: *Be a manifester for good.*

Manifester for good? So you want *us* to manifest good for you?

Gabriel: Not just for me. I want you to manifest good for you.

I thought "good" was an outlook. What's good to me may not be good to someone else. How would that work?

Gabriel: Manifest good for you, and in return, it will manifest what others think is good for them. It's all connected.

(This reminds me of the phrase "Do unto others as you would have them do unto you.")

I'm sorry, Gabriel, but I have other things on my mind at the moment that are getting in the way of this conversation. Can you help?

Gabriel: I will move those thoughts aside for you so we can get back into this channeling. Let me explain this lesson in further detail. Let's say that all you manifest is what you consider bad. Now, remember that life is a choice. You can continue to manifest what you consider bad if you want to. You have the free will to do that. But I don't want to see you continually manifest what you consider bad.

So manifest good. It's really that simple. I never want you to manifest things that you would consider bad or that are just poor choices in general for your overall life and health and everything about it. Choose to be grand always, in all ways. How you live your life is up to you, so since you have the freedom to do what you'd like, why would you want to manifest what is bad for you? Happiness is a choice, and you can learn your lessons in whatever way you choose to learn them, for you are the one creating them.

We are the ones creating the circumstances to learn our lessons? That isn't God/the Universe creating those circumstances?

Gabriel: You can go back to before you come to Earth for this life, to the moment where you choose all the lessons you want to learn as a spirit, a soul, on your upcoming journey as a human being. At that moment is when you decide what lessons you'd like to learn, and you choose an infinite number of ways to learn them.

When you get to the moment of being human, all of those options get "tossed in the air," and they are chosen by your choices and actions as you go throughout life. Your soul says, "OK, here is an opportunity to learn the lesson about faith," and then you proceed to learn that lesson in the way you are choosing to learn it.

If you decide as a human being that you choose to learn something else at that moment that is better suited for your current situation, then that lesson is learned. You aren't consciously choosing these lessons. This is all subconscious, for it comes from the soul, and your angels help you along the way. They are there to protect and guide you. What you think is an awful experience for someone else might be a lesson for them to learn because their spirit, their soul, chose that lesson regardless of how awful or amazing it is.

(The universe will keep putting us in situations to learn a certain lesson until we actually learn it. I also feel that even after we learn the lesson, we are placed back into that situation every once in a while to see how we handle it after learning it.)

Gabriel, that was incredible. I'm a bit speechless . . .

Gabriel: I know. It's awesome, isn't it?

I don't know if I'd use the word *awesome,* but it's definitely interesting. That completely knocked me out, and I don't know if I can handle another lesson this morning after that.

Gabriel: So it is. I will communicate with you tomorrow. Farewell, my friend.

Good morning, Gabriel. It's a beautiful day outside.

Gabriel: Is it a beautiful day inside as well?

Yes, it is. Are you hinting at something?

Gabriel: That depends. Would you like to hear another lesson?

That's why I'm channeling you.

(Take that, Gabriel. Ha!)

Gabriel: OK, good! The next lesson I want to teach you is: *Be happy inside.*

That seems simple enough. Please explain this in further detail, though, since I'm sure there's much more to it.

Gabriel: There is and there isn't. As I've taught you in previous lessons, how you feel inside is how your world looks outside. If you're miserable and sad inside, then that is how the world will look to you on the outside, and you will bring these subconscious thoughts into your world. If you're sad and miserable, then the world will show you a sad and miserable world and will bring those kinds of situations into your life to match your vibration. Remember, you are a vibration. You are energy. You are a magnet. Whatever you think about, you attract. That's it in a nutshell, Beau. The world is decided by your thoughts.

(This is getting good!)

The whole world is decided by *my* thoughts in particular?

Gabriel: To a certain extent, yes. Remember, what you see is what you get. The world is different to everybody. How you look at the world is *completely* different from how your mom looks at the world, for you are unique individuals with your own life experiences. No two people see the world the same. Your brains manufacture opinions differently from one another. You may have a lot of things in common and see the world similarly in certain areas, but know that you will *never* meet another human being who looks at the world identically to you, for it is impossible—just as there is no other human being identical to you. An identical twin isn't exactly the same as her sibling. Yes, they look a *lot* alike, but there are still many differences between them physically. No two human beings look identical, nor do two human beings *think* identically.

(This is why you may not see something in the same way somebody else does.)

In other words, we are all individuals.

Gabriel: When someone wants to mimic someone else, it's because they want to be like them and they aren't happy with whom they are in that area. Now, there is nothing wrong with following and mimicking someone's path if you're looking to get a similar outcome to what they got. You are learning from them, and in the process, you become your own unique version of them. You are now yourself.

Take this into the concept of when you started to make music. You wanted to sound like your favorite artist, so you did what he did in your own unique way. During that time, you were learning and forming your own individual version of him. This is what we call *influence*. You can be influenced by someone or something, but you should always be yourself. Being somebody or something else is not authentic.

So you're saying we should always be authentic? We can mimic others during the process of growing and learning, but in the end, we should be authentic and be ourselves. We shouldn't try to be someone or something that we're not.

Gabriel: Correct. Be you.

I knew there was so much more to this lesson of "be happy," for there are always many layers to the lessons you teach me. Is there anything else?

Gabriel: That is all. Live your day, and your life, [as] authentically as you possibly can, for you are only human.

I will. Thank you, Gabriel!

Gabriel: Remember, Beau. The only measure of success in life is looking in the mirror and accepting what you see. Work with what you have. You can make things work more efficiently, but always work with what you have because sometimes, you don't have a choice.

(Wow! There are things that come through me from Archangel Gabriel and Orion that knock me off my feet.)

That's powerful. I love it. Thank you, Gabriel.

How are you, Gabriel?

Gabriel: I'm great. You're great. Love is amazing. Serendipity resides in your heart and vocal chords as you project your voice to the world.

That's a new one. I haven't heard you say that one yet. So what is the next lesson you'd like to share with me?

Gabriel: *Confrontation* is a bad word.

I wanted to look up the definition of that word because of what you just said. The definition describes *confrontation* as "a hostile or argumentative meeting or situation between opposing parties." That said, I can see why you would say it's a bad word. I thought there was no such thing as "bad," though.

Gabriel: That is correct, Beau. There isn't, for there is no such thing as "bad." That's my point.

Explain this further, please, because I don't understand your point.

Gabriel: Sure. A confrontation is an argument between two parties. Arguing is barely even a conversation; all it really is, is a screaming match between two opposing parties. Remember, nothing gets resolved peacefully or efficiently or lovingly if confrontation is the reason for what is being said to resolve the issue. Human beings let their ego get in the way of what they really are, which is love. Love is what you are made of. It is what the Universe is made of. Ego has a tendency to come in very often for human beings and takes over love. When you fight, you are letting ego win. No one else wins—only ego.

So ego is the reason for confrontation?

Gabriel: That is correct. If love were the reason for confrontation, then it wouldn't be called a confrontation. It'd be called a love meeting. That isn't what is happening, though, in a confrontation. That said, the conversation could be about hurting other people. If it's done in a respectful way within the group that's meeting, then it isn't a confrontation. It doesn't matter what this meeting is about. It's more about how it's handled that defines it as a confrontation or meeting of love and respect. Two people or groups of people who are out to injure other people may speak to each other in a loving and respectful way regardless of the end result they are trying to accomplish. Do you get that the *reason* for the meeting is not the deciding factor as to whether or not it is a confrontation?

It definitely makes sense. A definition of a word is a definition of a word. It means what it means regardless of what I think it means or what you think it means.

(I really love "love meeting." I'm going to start using that. We could all start using that.)

Gabriel: Which brings me to the next lesson: *Only you decide what is "right" and "wrong."* Life is a choice, as I've told you many times before. The key here is to be OK with your choice. When you can accept what you consider "right" and "wrong," then you can be OK with what others think. Arguments over politics don't resolve anything. This again is all about ego. Edging God Out, as Wayne Dyer puts it. When you take away love and replace it with ego, you learn to be heartless and ruthless. You will do whatever it takes to prove your point. Be OK with another's opinion, for they understand life the way they do through their own experiences. This is how it is.

So if *confrontation* is a "bad" word, then can we say *ego* is a bad word?

> **Gabriel:** You tell me, Beau. Is it a bad word? Some people may not find *confrontation* to be a "bad" word.

You just told me it is a bad word through a life lesson!

> **Gabriel:** Remember that "good" and "bad" is nothing more than a point of view. Don't be mistaken by what I share with you. I say these things to make you think.

Well, you have me thinking.

> **Gabriel:** Good. I am happy about that then.

Is there anything else you'd like to share?

> **Gabriel:** That is all for this morning.

(The fact that everything is a choice is quite the eye-opener. It is a reminder that all of our decisions and how we feel about others' decisions is nothing more than a choice. It's such an easy concept to understand, but it's not always easy to accept, especially when it comes to other people's choices.)

Good morning, Gabriel. It's wonderful to channel you in the morning. What life lesson would you like to share with me today? By the way, how are you this morning?

(It just occurred to me I always ask this, as if I'm expecting that Archangel Gabriel is going to say something other than some form of "I'm incredible." I'm quite positive angels are always incredible.)

Gabriel: Beau, I am magical; I am always magical and happy. Remember, sadness and anger don't exist in an angel. The life lesson I'd like to share today is: *Arrogance is the familiarity of "bad."*

This is just like yesterday's lesson. I thought "bad" was all about perspective?"

Gabriel: It *is* perspective. When was the last time you met somebody who thought being arrogant was a good thing? Nobody likes arrogance. Therefore, it is a kind of perspective that a majority of the world perceives. Do you understand this?

I can definitely understand that, but what about people who *are* arrogant? Do they not like that arrogance displayed back to them?

Gabriel: Nobody wants to be treated rudely, even if they themselves are rude. They may not even realize they're rude. Take into account that nobody wants to be disrespected. This is why wars occur. This is why greed occurs. This is why arrogance occurs. You don't want to be offended, so you put up your guard and sometimes that guard is displayed as arrogance.

That's ironic. You can be arrogant to others, and maybe even aware of it, but the moment someone is arrogant back to you, it leaves you offended. We expect people to be nice even when we know we're being rude. When they act rude back to us, we're all like, "Wow, what a jerk!" and we act rudely and arrogantly right back. That's interesting to think about. There's nothing like throwing up a good guard, huh?

> **Gabriel:** That was funny, Beau, and a great observation. People aren't acting rudely back to *you* specifically. They are just protecting themselves from being offended and in return are being what you interpret as rude and arrogant back to you.

(This may be life changing to some readers. We may not even be aware that we're arrogant, and even if we are and it's pointed out to us by someone else, we may be offended by it. I feel that sometimes it is the perspective of the other person whether or not we come across as arrogant, and other times we really are arrogant and rude. But we have to realize it ourselves to change it. Remember, being arrogant or rude is a choice, just like being nice or kind is a choice.)

You're saying that they aren't being arrogant back to *us* specifically but rather because they are just putting up a defense mechanism and protecting themselves? We just happen to be in the way of their shield?

> **Gabriel:** That's what I am telling you, Beau. Don't take offense because even if it is pointed directly at you, it is not *about* you.

That seems to be so much easier said than done. It can be hard not to be offended by someone's rudeness. If I'm nice to you, then I expect you to be nice back. At the same time, I realize everyone carries their own history and stories throughout their life, and this is having them act a certain way.

> **Gabriel:** As long as you remember that it is *never* directed at *you* and *your* life specifically, then you can easily be with their communication. Life is a journey, Beau. Don't let others make you stumble along the way.

Well said, Gabriel. I like that line a lot. Is that everything? Is there more you'd like to share about this lesson?

Gabriel: No. That is all for this lesson and for today. Take care, Beau.

Bye, Gabriel. Thank you for everything.

(I was typing this channel out as I always do, and I accidently selected then deleted all of it. So much for technology improving our lives.)

Gabriel, I have to start this channel over. I lost everything. It wasn't a lot, but I didn't expect that to happen. Please share again what you were sharing with me about this new lesson.

> **Gabriel:** I wanted to make you aware that you need to always plan ahead. Save the file often. Save yourself often when it comes to planning your life. Remember I was telling you about setting a schedule, or at least making a list of things to do. Don't rely on your memory. Leave space in your memory for certain things—make a list or schedule of what needs to get done and create priorities. Once a week, sit down and create your schedule, and make a list of those things you want to do the night before. If you don't feel like you have time, then you should *definitely* do this.
>
> All of this goes back to the lesson of *you* being the creator of your life. Remember in the film *The Secret*, Joe Vitale shared that you can write down what you want? Do that. This is what I am telling you that you can do when it comes to a schedule. You choose how your life goes. Now, just because you write it down doesn't mean that it will magically appear, if you aren't doing anything to achieve it. Once you create that schedule, make a list of things to do for that day and *do them*.
>
> Beau, this that I am sharing is only of importance if you want to have what you want. If it isn't important enough to you, you will find an excuse not to do it. Your life is in your hands. It's not in mine, nor is it in God's hands. The worst thing you can do to yourself is promise yourself something and then not do anything to have it. This is just as bad if you create a schedule to achieve

it and then don't follow it. I understand that things will change and look different, but if that happens, you can still achieve your goals. If it switches midway, then that is great. Follow your goals. Follow your dreams. Follow your heart. Follow your love.

That was incredible. Unfortunately, I have to end this conversation.

(I did a lot of self-development work during the time of these channels, and a lot of things that are mentioned relate to what I learned. Setting a schedule is one of those things. At the time, the things I learned felt as if they were geared toward me and my life. I'm realizing nearly two and a half years later that these are for everybody. Setting a schedule is completely related to taking 100 percent responsibility for our life.)

Good morning, Gabriel. What is the next life lesson you'd like to share with me?

Gabriel: *Tampering with your plan will only cause it to take more time.*

Take more time to . . .

Gabriel: It'll take more time to come to fruition. Remember that your plan is decided by you. This goes back to what we just talked about regarding creating a schedule. If you don't follow that schedule, things will take longer to happen. That's life. That's how the world works. Plan it and execute it. It's as simple as that. God had an idea for the universe, so God created the universe. God did not wait. God planned everything and created. Remember that God is perfect. God and the universe (which, in essence, is the same thing) are perfect. The planet Earth is perfect. *You* are created perfectly to be who you are supposed to be in the life you live.

What does your listing all those things that are perfect have to do with this lesson?

Gabriel: When it comes to you planning out your life, I want you to remember that things won't ever go as planned. That doesn't mean you won't achieve your results. That just means the Universe will bring you the outcome you want differently than you expected. Isn't that super amazing? There is an infinite number of paths you can take. You choose one of those plans when you write it out, and then the Universe decides a better way for you to get to the end result.

So, we aren't *really* in control. The Universe is in control. In other words, are we really controlling our life, as you keep telling me?

Gabriel: What is control? You decide. You make choices.

Haven't you always used the words "You control your life?"

Gabriel: There is a lesson here I want you to get. That lesson is this: *You type what you decide to hear.* I give you the idea and you then type it out because you are deciding how to hear it. Does this make sense?

Yes, it does.

Gabriel: OK, good. That means that no matter what I say to you, you will interpret it how you choose to hear it. The Universe sees the choices you make and then works in tandem with you to quickly achieve those goals. If your plans can be done in a quicker and/or different way than you planned, then it will guide you into that region of your life.

The Universe likes speed. Everything moves at a speed unmeasured by humans. Isn't that so cool to think about? Remember that Joe Vitale from *The Secret* film I recently mentioned says that the Universe likes speed. Don't doubt yourself and hesitate. Plan and execute. It's like the conversation you had with your friend recently. You are already powerful. You just have to remember that and then be that. Also, realize that you are *already being* powerful. You just need to be reminded. Strength comes from within. Once you remember that you're strong and powerful, you can then act that way.

(I see this as a wake-up call to humanity. We are already powerful. We just have to accept it and, more importantly, own it.)

This is a very eye-opening conversation. Thank you for sharing this. Is there anything else you'd like to add to this conversation?

Gabriel: That is all for today. Remember that you are already great, so you can live your life in that state of mind.

It is beautiful to communicate, Gabriel. Channeling you never gets old. It is always a joyous moment.

> **Gabriel:** So it is for me. Would you like me to enchant you with a new lesson of life?

Yes, I would. What is the next lesson?

> **Gabriel:** Be *enchanting*. In other words, remember that you already possess the ability of enchanting others. Come from that space and live as that. There really is no such thing as "be," for you already are. *Be* and *are*. *Beare*. Now look at the similarity in spelling between that and *bear*. To bear something means to support something. Support yourself. Support others by being and also by remembering you *are* whatever you want to be already. There is no *be*. You *are* what you say.

(I've been writing song lyrics since '94 or '95, and I've always been big on wordplay. This makes it so fun and special when Archangel Gabriel plays with words.)

That was cool. I love when you play with words like that. You say we *are* what we say. If there is no such thing as "be" since we already "are," then if we say we are weak, we already have that in us?

> **Gabriel:** Why would you want to use *weak* as an example? You are powerful. Don't *be* powerful. Remember that you *are* powerful. It is already in you. Everything is already in you, from the "good" to the "bad."

(Don't be *powerful. You already* are *powerful. That is the difference between* be *and* are. *I feel like to* be *something means to act "as if" from that moment on—but it is still an act. When you* are *something, you own it.)*

If that's the case, what else is there to share about this lesson? Is there even anything?

Gabriel: Consider we are only scratching the surface of your potential.

Our potential for what? I thought I learned once (maybe not from you) that there is no such thing as potential. Can you clarify all of this?

Gabriel: Human beings, at least most, feel like they have limits. They feel they can only do things to a certain extent. This is not true. Neil Armstrong set numerous world records. Michael Jordan became the greatest basketball player of all time according to most. Stephen Hawking got to experience weightlessness on a parabolic flight. People with no limbs do things daily that people with limbs don't believe they can do. You are right that *potential* is a made-up idea. It puts limits on you [to say], "You have the potential to be great." You already *are* great. Don't ever forget this. There are no limits. You are the only thing that ever holds you back from anything. If Stephen Hawking, a paraplegic, can float in zero gravity and someone with no limbs can be a motivational speaker, then you can do *anything*. Stop putting limits on yourself. That's not fair to your being.

That is because our being can achieve anything.

Gabriel: Don't doubt.

This is really powerful, to be told that we have *no* limits, even if we think we do.

(We are limitless! It is shared time and time again by Archangel Gabriel that we are so much more powerful than we realize. This, to me, is confirmation.)

Gabriel: You can learn to sing. You can learn to dance. You can learn to be great at basketball. I never said it would be easy. What

I am saying is that you can do *anything*. It takes a strong mindset, which every individual has. You put limits on yourself and let your past dictate who you are instead of letting your present dictate who you are. If you are everything, that means that your soul is everything, which means that your soul is the present moment. Realize this and you can have it all.

After you said that, I began thinking about how this whole world in front of our eyes is made up. We are individually creating it. What I see out my window may be similar to what someone else sees, but it is not identical. If we are making everything up moment by moment, then we can create whatever we want. It is time to create!

Gabriel: Go get'em, Beau!

I will. Thank you, Gabriel. Is there anything else you'd like to share?

Gabriel: This is it for today. I wanted you to get what you got. Take care.

Ha. Bye, Gabriel.

Good morning, Gabriel. How are you?

Gabriel: Beau, you ask me this all of the time, and I always give you the same answer. I am magnificent. If you are expecting me to say anything different, then you are not listening. This goes right into the next lesson: *Listen to how others talk about themselves.* You can always tell how genuine they are when they say something. Your gut always knows the answer.

This goes back to trusting your instincts. The internal messenger can always [differentiate] truth from fiction. Allow your body to speak to you and allow yourself to really listen. There is only time to listen. Once you stop listening to others speak, you will stop listening to the truth of nature. The fortified delivery of life is elegant and blissful, for the only opportunity to speak clarity is to evolve into the brand of nature that is realistic in your reality.

What? You seem to have strayed completely off course and away from the conversation we were having about trusting our instincts and listening to others. What does the "fortified delivery of life" have to do with that?

Gabriel: There is always a connection, Beau. Please remember this, for I do not speak to you about anything other than the lesson I am teaching, or rather reminding, you about. The fortified delivery of life is a strengthened delivery of life. This delivery is powerful. It is a powerful delivery of life that is elegant and blissful, for the only opportunity to speak clarity is to evolve into the brand of nature that is realistic in your reality. Is this making sense to you?

(Before we go on, I feel what Archangel Gabriel means by "fortified delivery of life" is to be strong enough mentally and emotionally to protect your thoughts and feelings about something you find important. I feel the whole paragraph above is referring to how important it is to own your ways of being. You own your thoughts. You own your life. You own what you create. You own who you are. You can only speak clearly about something when you own it. For example, if you know about math to the point you can share it easily, own that you know it because when you own that you know it, you are confident in what you say.)

It kind of is, but not really. Please continue to clarify.

> **Gabriel:** I can do that. That's the goal. I want you to consider that the "brand of nature that is realistic in your reality" is just another way of saying that the world that you live in is created only by *you*, and how you view the world will determine the strength of your instincts when it comes to learning the truth about who people are at their core. So to clarify, listen to your instincts because your instincts are created by the way you have lived your life. They are always correct and will always lead you the right way, even if your thoughts and ego disagree. If you have a feeling about something that is so strong that you can't disengage it from your emotions, then you are correct in your feelings.

You have such a way with words, Gabriel. I am always fascinated by your way of communicating to me.

> **Gabriel:** I also want to share something else that I see you do a lot during our conversations, something you picked up on in the conversation that we're having. There is a difference between *speaking* and *communicating*. Speaking is an action. Communicating is based on feeling and clarity. Also, there is a difference between what is "right" and what is "correct." "Right" as well as "wrong" are choices and decisions you make. When something is correct, it is the truth. There is also a difference in how you use the word

truth. *True* and *false* are decisions and choices. Truth is simply what is correct. Do you see the connection? There is a difference.

I like how you used those words together. So "truth" is not necessarily "right," but it is correct. It is so interesting to look at it that way. Thank you for sharing that with me. Is there anything else you'd like to share regarding all of that?

Gabriel: Yes, there is one more thing. The Truth will set you free. It will always lead you home. Home is in the soul. It is in the spirit. You reach it in your mind while on this plane that we call Earth. There is no other way to say that other than you are loved. Be all that you can be, and also remember that you already are. You just have to be reminded.

We have to be reminded that we already are?

Gabriel: Yes, that is correct.

Thank you, Gabriel, for such beautiful words.

Gabriel, it's wonderful to have you here with me. Is there anything you'd like to say before we move on to the next lesson?

Gabriel: Your messages will be passed down through generations of people to the point that they will become lessons taught in school. Don't ever doubt your power. Also, don't doubt if you will come back as a child who learns these things that are being taught in school.

(These lessons will be taught in school?! I'm getting a free education. I wonder if Archangel Gabriel will want royalties. Ha!)

Well, I was told I am ninety lives deep. How many more lives will I be going through?

Gabriel: Beau, you don't have to know everything.

(We all have past lives. We experience life as a human being a lot in different lives and different moments of time. Some people have lived more lifetimes than others, but just because they've lived more lives than you doesn't mean they are more special. Their spirit just chose to learn a lot, or they haven't yet learned all the lessons they've wanted to learn.)

All right, fair enough. So what is the next life lesson you'd like to share with me?

Gabriel: Out of all the lessons, I want everyone to really pay attention to this one. *The only criminal act in this universe is to be somebody else's perspective.* What I mean by this is, become who *you* want to become. Don't be what someone else is saying you should be. At the moment, you can realize this and change the direction you're heading; if you're going down that path, the more enjoyable your life will be as time goes on.

In other words, be ourselves. Be *you.*

Gabriel: I'm so happy you understand this. Here is another lesson that follows along with that: *Enjoy life how you see it.*

What if we see it with a cynical view?

Gabriel: Then choose that and enjoy the world through a cynical view. Remember, *you* may think it's cynical, but the person who's looking at the world that way may not think so. What I am saying is that if you are looking at your life through a cynical filter (and again, "cynical" is a perspective because what is cynical to you may not be cynical to someone else), enjoy and embrace that cynical filter with all your heart. When you learn a new way to look at life, embrace that new way. If you choose to view life through that new filter, embrace that and smile. It's all a choice. You can be cynical and still be happy. It's hard— and it is possible.

Isn't "hard" a perspective?

Gabriel: That is correct. How do you want to live your life?

I want to live my life happy and peacefully.

Gabriel: Then all you have to do is choose that.

It all comes back to choice, as you've said many times before. That's great to be reminded of. Is there anything else you'd like to share about this lesson, or is there another lesson?

(It's wild to me that so many of the lessons come down to the same thing: choice. Almost everything we do and experience comes down to choice. That's what I'm understanding. This means that we have a choice how to live life and how we react to events that happen in our life. It's also going back to taking 100 percent responsibility for our life.)

Gabriel: There is nothing left for me to communicate.

I guess that means it's time to end this channeling for today. Take care, Gabriel, and thank you.

Gabriel: Good-bye, Beau. Shine on.

Good morning, Gabriel. It's nice to communicate with you first thing in the morning. It's a great way to start my day.

Gabriel: If only you knew how amazing it is for me to be with you in the morning or anytime, you would be floored.

I can't even imagine. What new life lesson can you share with me today?

Gabriel: I like this one a lot. Are you ready? *The choice to be persistent defines what your life looks like in your future.*

Well, the wording is interesting, but I think I can get the point you're trying to make.

Gabriel: Remember, Beau, there is no "try."

I know there isn't. I just didn't know how else to say that. I realize you aren't "trying" to do anything. What you're saying is that our life will look different if we are persistent with something, compared to if we are not persistent with something. For instance, if I'm persistent about a career I want, I will do whatever it takes to get it, regardless of how many times I get turned down during the journey to get there. Now, I realize it may not look how I imagined it in my head, but I can still have it if I am persistent. What I did get in the midst of typing is that it comes down to a "whatever it takes" mentality, which I feel is the main thing you want to point out to me. Am I correct about this?

Gabriel: Yes, you are. Do whatever it takes to have your dreams come true. There is no "try." You either do or you don't. It's really that simple. Don't ever doubt yourself, because that just stops you.

(Go after your dreams.)

Point noted. Is there anything else you'd like to share about this lesson, or is there another lesson you'd like to share with me?

Gabriel: No, Beau, there is nothing. Take this lesson into your life today and remember you are already powerful. There is no need to *be* powerful. Just remember you already are and take on life from there. Don't let little things defeat you. Take on Life now.

I will, Gabriel. Thank you so much.

Good morning, Gabriel. How's the family?

Gabriel: You know the family is everyone, every spirit and soul and everything. That said, the family is perfection.

Being that perfection doesn't exist in human reality and *does* exist in the spirit world, I believe that your family is perfection. We are the perfect versions of ourselves, the Universe is perfect, and the Earth is perfect, from nature to the animals to the sea creatures. Everything is perfect exactly how it is. Is this a correct understanding of it?

Gabriel: It is. That was a great job explaining that. Let's move on to the next lesson with that in mind: *The campaign of thought relies on the sight of the manifester.*

That took a few seconds to figure out, but I think I understand it. What you're saying is that the one who is manifesting brings about what he sees in his mind. So if I wanted to see success in romance, I would have to picture it all in my mind before taking physical action *and* I'd have to follow through with it in physical reality to see it come true. Am I getting this correct?

Gabriel: You are getting it correct to a certain extent. This really goes back to the point of you creating your whole world. You create *everything* through thought. Remember this as I continue with the teaching of this lesson. The world is created by human beings. God gave you a blank canvas to work on. It is now your turn to create. You are God in human form, which means you are energy in human form. You are a manifester. Manifest! You are already incredible. Remember this when you are creating, for you can truly create anything. There is no guidance system stronger than your intuition. Listen to it because that is the Universe talking to you. Listen to your instincts because they are *always* right.

(I've learned over my life that just because we see it a certain way in our mind doesn't mean that we will want it exactly that way. When we receive it in real life the same way as we see it in our mind, we may not want it that way after all. We are continually changing our mind until we are truly happy and we receive what we really want.)

I was just thinking of what a great meaning would be for GPS: God's Path Seen.

> **Gabriel:** That is beautiful. I gave that to God, as well as angels, as well as you.

So to break it down, we create. Our intuition is always right, so we should listen to it. In other words, trust it. Is this correct?

> **Gabriel:** Absolutely it is. You nailed it!

(I am totally patting myself on the back right now.)

Is there anything else you'd like to share?

> **Gabriel:** I'm not going anywhere. I know you worry. I am here to stay unless you absolutely tell me to leave, which I don't see you doing.

I don't plan on it. Thank you for this gift. It is incredible to have your intelligence at a moment's notice.

Hello, my dear Gabriel. You dove into the light like it was water and swam down to me. I've never seen you do that before. Was there a reason for that?

> **Gabriel:** *Dive into the pool of life.* That's the next lesson I want to share with you.

That's a cool lesson! Isn't *want* one of *those* words, though? I want this. I want that. It's not something that declares a necessity. Even if I said, "I *need* this" or "I *need* that," it still isn't a necessity. That's purely an observation. We don't "need" anything, and it's never a necessity to have the things we want. That's an observation, an opinion. Am I right about that?

> **Gabriel:** You are absolutely correct about all of that. You aren't "right." You are correct. Remember, life is an observation. Life is a choice. It is your *choice* to want. It is your observation to need. Neither of those words declares the next word a necessity. If you want to be happy, then God, the Universe, will give that to you. Now what? Are you really happy? Do you want more? See, the thing about human beings is that there is not always a necessity for necessities. There are a lot of humans who only want or feel the need. "If only I had this, life would be perfect." That's an observation and is not necessarily true.

How can we tell the difference between a want/need and a necessity?

> **Gabriel:** Believe that the answer is inside you. There Is only so much I can share with you because you really need to be taught how to trust your instincts. You have to trust your intuition. Your intuition knows the truth. It knows what you really do

have to acquire to create the satisfaction that comes from having a necessity.

So to go back to the actual lesson you shared, "Dive into the pool of life," what can you share about that lesson with me?

Gabriel: Take that literally. "Dive into the pool of life" is another way of saying to take on life head-on. Go for the gold. There is nothing to fear but fear itself, and you are in control of your life.

That's something you've been teaching me for a long time. If we are in control of our life, then take it on headfirst. Dive into the pool of life and grind. Go for the gold. That lesson seems easy enough to understand. Is there more to it than what I just said?

Gabriel: No, there is not, for I am here to give you reminders and help you lead the best life possible.

That sounds good. Is there anything you'd like to share with me about this lesson, and if not, is there another lesson you'd like to share with me today?

Gabriel: There is no other lesson for today. We actually talked about a lot when taking your first question into consideration. We helped get you clear on something important for everyone to understand. That share will help you take on Life head-on.

That's great. Thank you, Gabriel. Bye!

Gabriel: Bye, Beau, and remember to dive into Life headfirst!

(I feel that the idea of taking on life head-on and that we are in control of our life leads back to the repeated saying of taking 100 percent responsibility. It's such a strong message because it is so important for us as human beings to get.)

What's up, Gabriel?

Gabriel: What is up, Beau? I see you are speaking to me the way you speak with everybody. It's about time you were more yourself during these channelings.

You say that as if you were happy about that.

Gabriel: I have always shared with you to be yourself. Be *you*. Don't worry about how others see you and judge you. That's their own choice, which is why I bring all of this up for the next lesson I will share with you, which is tied into this: *The absolute certainty of Life is to be a communication of your reflection in the mirror.*

Can we simplify that to a simple "Be yourself?"

Gabriel: Who you see yourself to be is who you broadcast to the world. You broadcast it to the universe. Don't ever be something you are not, for you will be cheating yourself out of a human right.

It is a human right to be our Self?

Gabriel: Yes, it is. It is truly the only human right. Be Your Self always in all ways, for what you bring to the planet is what is reflected back to you. Think of the Earth and the Universe as mirrors. They work with you to bring you what you see in your mind. If you believe you are a superstar, the Universe will reflect that back to you. Always be your best and always be yourself. There are no mistakes in this universe. Everything happens for a reason, even if you think differently. Truth is truth, as your mother says. There is no right or wrong, for that is a choice. There is just Truth. There is *only* Truth.

(I love that Archangel Gabriel says, "Think of the Earth and Universe as mirrors." What we see in our mind, what we think, and what we feel creates our world. If we are the Universe in human form, then it makes complete sense for us to see the Universe and Earth as mirrors. They are reflections of us.)

Are you saying, then, that there is no such thing as a lie?

> **Gabriel:** There is only Truth. A lie is another way of explaining an untruth.

That's an interesting way of looking at it. There is no right or wrong, for that is a choice, and what is right to somebody may be wrong to somebody else. I can't say the same thing about truth because truth is truth. That's just how the Universe works.

> **Gabriel:** You are correct. Truth and saying something is correct are interchangeable forms of communication that explain the same thing.

Communication, you recently said, is different from *speaking,* correct?

> **Gabriel:** Speaking is definitely not the same as communicating. What you speak may not be a form of communication. Do you understand this?

I do. If I yell at you, that isn't necessarily communicating with you. Same goes if I say to you, "You're ugly." That's a view I have, and that view isn't truth. It's all interchangeable, and it all comes back to what is Truth and what is not.

> **Gabriel:** There really isn't even a "false," for it is either true or untrue. The word *false* is another choice we make. If you tell someone he is ugly, that isn't true, for that is your view. If you tell him he's ugly and he responds, "That is false," that is *his* own view. There is no "ugly" in this world, for everything is based on your view. It is based on your life experience. Truth is truth. God

is God is God is God is God. That is true. You are a human being. That is true. You are ugly. That is untrue. It is not false, for saying it is false is a personal decision. This doesn't mean you *are*, though. Do you understand this?

(This reminds me of the popular phrase "Beauty is in the eye of the beholder.")

I do understand this. That is really fascinating to look at it this way. Is there anything else you'd like to share about this lesson?

Gabriel: Just be yourself, and don't worry about what other people think. You are you, and that is all that matters. The only Truth regarding that is that you are you.

That seems to be easy enough. Is there another lesson you'd like to share with me this morning?

Gabriel: No, there is not.

Thank you, Gabriel.

Good morning, Gabriel. As I was going through the process of channeling you, I started to get thoughts that today's life lesson would be about consistency. Is this correct?

Gabriel: To a certain extent, yes, it is. Today's lesson is: *Be aware of your thoughts and dictation.* Procrastination will get you nowhere except for the places you don't want to be. In other words, you'll be stuck in the same place you were before, and by "same place," I mean emotionally and physically (to an extent.)

If you want anything in this life, you have to stay consistent in your actions to get to where you want to be. Dictate your life how you choose. You are the creator of your life. Remember this sentence: You create your life moment by moment. The result of your life is dictated by how you think about yourself. If you think you are worthy of what you want and have no hesitation about it, then it will appear in your physical world. If you know you deserve only the best but constantly question whether you're worth it or not, then it won't appear. You have to work at it and you have to believe it'll happen, no matter *what.* Obstacles will appear along your path. They always do. Stay consistent. Stay positive and keep your eyes on the goal. Keep your eyes on the prize. Have you ever noticed that a lot of common sayings that have been around forever seem to be true? "Keep your eyes on the prize" is one of many.

I have noticed that. I imagine that a human said it, and it was inspired by Spirit.

Gabriel: It always is, isn't it?

(I really feel it's more than just quotes here and there. It can also go for song lyrics, art, and even this!)

Indeed, this is true. Is there anything else you'd like to share?

Gabriel: That is all, for I'd like for you to rest.

Thank you. Take care, Gabriel.

Gabriel: I will. I am always well.

Hello there, Gabriel. I've started to take notice of that big smile I get when you enter. Seeing it in the mirror is wild because it's the biggest smile I can make.

> **Gabriel:** You know why, Beau? It's because all I am is happy. Angels are all happy. We all have giant smiles on our faces.

I thought you didn't have faces, that you're just a ball of energy.

> **Gabriel:** That depends how you see us. If you saw us in a physical form, we'd have giant smiles on our faces.

That's awesome! So what lesson would you like to share with me today, Gabriel?

> **Gabriel:** *Be yourself* has been taught to you numerous times. What I will add to that is *be exclusively you.*

(In other words, be yourself. I love that phrase, though.)

That's a unique lesson. We should be ourselves and be ourselves exclusively?

> **Gabriel:** If you were to be yourself, then how could you be anyone else and why would you want to be anyone else? The purpose of being yourself is to be who you are. Being someone else is of no service to learning who you are at your best. Be gracious.

I definitely wouldn't want to be anyone else. In fact, your teachings have really taught me to accept myself and who I am, especially when it comes to my music. I always tried to sound like somebody else, and I've realized recently that I just need to be me.

(I wish I had learned this earlier with regard to making my own music. In life, we can be influenced by certain people, but it is for our best and highest good to be ourselves.)

Gabriel: I have noticed this and I am happy about that; hence, the big smile on my face.

You're funny. What else would you like to share about this lesson, if anything?

Gabriel: Just be you, and be only you forever in your life. Being someone else doesn't serve you. You must learn to accept who you are, for you will gain the most success when you do.

Isn't *must* one of those words that's a choice but not a necessity?

Gabriel: Good observation. I say to you that you must. That doesn't mean it's the right thing to do. Even "right" is one of those judgmental words. Do you understand what I am getting at?

I think so. We don't *have* to accept who we are, but why would we not?

Gabriel: See, life is a choice, as I've told you many times before. Choices make your world go round.

Choose this. Choose that. It's all about choosing. Is there anything else?

Gabriel: This is all for this lesson.

Take care, Gabriel and, forevermore, thank you. I'm getting there is one more thing you'd like to share?

Gabriel: Yes, there is. The opportunity to be yourself happens at every single moment of your life. Take advantage of that.

I will. Thank you, Gabriel.

Good morning, Gabriel. How are you, and what new lesson do you have for me today?

Gabriel: I am amazing this morning and always in all ways. Today's lesson is: *The misconception that life is decided by others.* The lesson here is to believe in you.

We should believe in our own power? Is that what you're saying?

Gabriel: Yes, that is exactly what I'm saying. Believe in *you*. When you believe in yourself, your whole world will change. Things will start to work out, and when they don't work out the first time you try them, then it will make it easier for you to try something else until it's completed.

That makes sense. We are capable of anything.

Gabriel: You are, but you don't realize that all the time—or at all, for most. Be the power you are. It's a matter of remembering, just like it's a matter of remembering you are infinite. All of these lessons are supposed to help you remember. These lessons aren't meant for me to share with you to be this or be that.

Is there anything else you'd like to share about this lesson?

Gabriel: Just remember where you came from because when you do, it will all make sense to you.

Thanks, Gabriel.

Good morning, Gabriel. What lesson would you like to share with me today?

Gabriel: The life lesson I'd like to share with you today is to *be of service not only to others but to yourself.* Take care of yourself. Others taking care of themselves would benefit them so much. Physical, mental, and emotional health is so important to a healthy lifestyle. A healthy mind and body trumps everything. Working out or even just taking a walk every day, as well as meditating even if only for five minutes, will reflect back onto you and then back onto the rest of your life and the rest of the world. Silence yourself for a few minutes and focus on a peaceful you.

(I am clear that everything that is for our best and highest good as a human being is easy, like exercising, eating healthy, and meditating. I don't feel that you have to break your back.)

My mom always says that people think it takes work to meditate, when all you have to do is close your eyes and breathe. Why would God make something so important so hard to do? It's an easy task.

Gabriel: She is correct. All of the things that it takes to be healthy are easy things to do. All you have to do is walk for a bit. Walking around every day, doing your normal life, isn't necessarily enough, especially if you are sitting in front of a desk all day. Also, eating healthily and clean isn't a task. Yes, it'll take some work at the very beginning, getting clear about what is clean and what isn't, and really focusing on your health. The beginning is always the toughest in regard to anything in life you do.

Everything gets easier to accomplish over time, if you do it consistently. Remember you are strong. Remember you are smart. Remember you are already healthy. There is a healthy person underneath the stress, the extra weight, and the emotions. You are made in the image and likeness of God, which is the spirit and soul that you are. You have come here to the planet Earth in human form, for it is the most functional ship to guide you throughout life. Remember that your body can do anything and that your brain and mind can do anything. Wish it, dream it, and do it, as the sign says in your studio.

(I turned my office into a small home recording studio, and I have that sign Gabriel mentioned hanging in it. I'm all about motivation.)

All of that is easier said than done, though.

Gabriel: Breaking down the barriers is a lesson to learn in life for everyone.

That is powerful. Why *is* it so difficult for most people to break through a lot of things?

Gabriel: There is a lesson in everything, and when you learn that you can *do* anything and everything, that's when Life becomes astonishing. You'll learn that you can do whatever you want. *You can do whatever it takes. It just takes discipline.* That right there is another lesson, and more of an extension of the one I just shared. It just takes discipline, which is connected to the very first thing we talked about. We can even extend the idea of discipline to dedication. You must dedicate yourself to whatever you want to accomplish, for it takes discipline to *stay* dedicated.

Discipline is that important to success, huh?

Gabriel: Yes, it is; it is one of the biggest lessons for a lot of people to get. Don't give up if you can help it. Even when obstacles come your way, which they will, maneuver around them the best you can. Life is all about experience. Remember, God is *experiencing* Life *through* you.

(I think about someone like Stephen Hawking, who studies space at levels possibly deeper than anyone although he can hardly move his body due to his illness. The fact he can study something so complex so deeply, even with his physical limits, makes him unstoppable in my eyes.)

And God wouldn't have put limits on us so we couldn't do something.

Gabriel: Let's be clear about that. Some people do have physical and emotional "limits." It's a matter of breaking those limits, for limits are only in the mind. We've discussed this before.

You're right. I believe we have. Is there anything else you'd like to share regarding these lessons, or is there another lesson you'd like to share?

Gabriel: That is it for now. Review and conquer.

Hey there, Gabriel. How are you?

Gabriel: I am wonderful, but you seem to be somewhat upset.

If you're talking about the AC guy showing up during the last hour of his four-hour window, then yes.

(This is all tied to the lesson that Archangel Gabriel shares a little farther down.)

Gabriel: Don't be. Plus, I'd like to remind you that it is a choice.

Thank you for that reminder. It was definitely needed. I wanted to channel you earlier this morning, and I didn't want him to show up in the middle of the channeling

Gabriel: The thought came to you that he wouldn't show up during it. Why didn't you trust that thought?

It didn't seem to come from you or any other angel. It very much seemed like my own thoughts. Is all of this related to the lesson you will be sharing with me today?

Gabriel: That's for you to decide. Today's lesson is to *be aware of your present thoughts*.

I thought we shouldn't "be" anything.

Gabriel: There is so much more to understand. When I say "be" in this lesson, it is to help you remember the awareness you have of your past thoughts. They are always there. Some people decide to hide them to protect themselves.

That's a great observation, Gabriel. So we could become aware of our ... wait a minute. You just first said, "present thoughts," and then said, "past thoughts." I'm confused now. Please clear this up.

> **Gabriel:** Your present thoughts are your past thoughts the moment you have them. Remember, there is only the Now. So there is either Now, or there is the past. The past and the future do not exist, so there is truly only the Now. That is all. *Past* and *future* are made-up dialect for the human brain to understand the differences.

I understand the point you're making, and I'm confused. I'm having trouble focusing on this channeling today.

> **Gabriel:** Perfect. Be aware of your present thoughts. Close your eyes, breathe deeply a few times, and let go of any worries and concerns and stressors that are keeping you unbalanced. Return to me when you're ready.

(I do what Archangel Gabriel suggests.)

OK, I'm back. I don't know how long I was doing that for. I didn't check the time before I closed my eyes.

> **Gabriel:** If I told you that you were out for twelve minutes, would you believe me?

Who else am I to believe?

> **Gabriel:** Believe in yourself. We can add this to the lesson I just taught: *Be aware of your present thoughts and believe in yourself.*

I am not necessarily seeing how they are connected, though something tells me they are.

> **Gabriel:** Believe in yourself, Beau. This is what the whole lesson is about. Be aware of your present thoughts and believe in yourself.

I will do that, Gabriel. Is there anything else you'd like to share regarding this lesson, or is there another lesson you'd like to share?

Gabriel: Do you believe there is?

No, I don't. Am I correct?

Gabriel: Yes, you are correct. Be great, Beau.

Thank you, Gabriel. You, too.

(Trust your intuition. After about two years of doing this myself, I've learned my feelings are usually correct.)

Gabriel, how are you this morning?

Gabriel: I'm fancy and chipper. How are you?

I'm great, Gabriel. Thanks. What life lesson would you like to share with me today?

Gabriel: *Accept yourself for who you are always, in all ways, for there is never a moment when you are not you.* There is only you being you. You can act like somebody else, but you are you when you wake up and when you go to sleep. Accept yourself and the rest will follow.

These last few lessons have been about ourselves: accepting ourselves, being ourselves, being of service to ourselves . . . Why are you sharing all of this? What is the big lesson here?

Gabriel: The big lesson here, Beau, is to know you are on a journey where you are the only vehicle you will ever be driving. At no point in life will you be able to transfer to somebody else's vehicle. The body you have is the only one you will be transporting yourself in throughout your entire life. Accept your body, love your body, and serve your body so it operates to the best of its ability.

That's easy to say to someone who is blessed to have all of his limbs and every body part functioning extremely well. What about those who are paralyzed from the waist down or even the neck down? What about those who are brain-dead? What about those with no limbs? What do you have to say about that?

Gabriel: Remember that Life is a choice and you can operate at any level you choose. Yes, some people have those occurrences about them. It is their choice as to how they operate with those circumstances. Those who are brain-dead do not have a choice about how to operate. They were left with what they had before they went brain-dead. Also realize that in such cases, even though the body is operating the way it is, the soul is usually gone.

(What I feel happens to those who are brain-dead, in a coma but still moving or something similar, is that their spirit made a choice to come to earth with this situation as something they'd experience. It is a choice from the other side, but it is still a choice. This tells you how important choices are to our lives.)

I know *I* understand that. I don't know how many other people who will read this will understand that, especially if they don't believe in the same things I believe in.

Gabriel: That is not for you to worry about. Those who get it will get it, and those who don't want to accept it won't accept it. That's fine, Beau. There is no need for you to worry about that. Share this information the way I share it with you and it will be understood by some and not understood by others. Those who don't want to accept what I say or who don't understand the lessons I am relaying are just as intelligent as you are. There is nothing "wrong" with those people. Everyone is on his own journey, with his own life experiences and [his] own values. Don't judge others, ever. There is no need, and you are only judging yourself because they are a reflection of you.

Well said, Gabriel. You kind of put me in my place with that. I don't think that was intentional, though.

Gabriel: I would never be mean-spirited to you. I hope you realize this. I will be humorous with you but never mean-spirited.

OK, good. Is that everything you'd like to share for this lesson, or is there anything else?

Gabriel: That is all for today, Beau. Take these lessons and share them.

Indeed, I will. Thank you, Gabriel.

Hello there, Gabriel. I feel so at peace when I channel you.

Gabriel: Isn't that great? You can have that all the time. Once you come to that sense of peace internally, you can express it eternally. It's amazing, really.

(About two and a half years later, I am normally at peace; feeling like this will definitely change your life for the better, in my opinion.)

I imagine our soul is naturally at peace.

Gabriel: Your spirit is. Your soul can feel emotion and be emotional. Your essence, your spirit, is forever connected to Source, even more so than the soul. You're all connected, and the spirit is just a little bit more deeply connected than the soul is. Not by a lot, though enough to not feel the emotions of anger, depression, or mistrust.

That is really something to think about. I didn't even know it was like that. Thank you for sharing that. Is that what today's life lesson is all about?

Gabriel: It's part of it. Here is today's lesson: *Patience is more important than illusion.*

Is that another way of saying that patience to see what we picture in our mind to manifest is more important than what we actually picture? I know that nothing happens instantly. I mean, I guess it can, depending on how connected we actually are, but most of the time, we have to be patient to see our manifestation come to reality.

Gabriel: You got it. I'm happy about that. Stick to trusting yourself and your integrity, for the fall of your own empire is in your hands. When things don't go as planned, that is when your patience wears thin. Don't be disillusioned.

You mean that literally, don't you?

Gabriel: I do mean that literally. Don't be disillusioned when your illusion doesn't go exactly how you pictured it, because it *never* does. The road to success is never complete. It is always a work in progress. You learned that the other day.

(It is strangely comforting that the road to success is never complete. If only I had realized this at the time I channeled it. I'd have been so much easier on myself and would have stopped trying to get things "perfect.")

I did, so I'm glad it was confirmed just now. Is there anything else you'd like to share regarding this lesson, or is there another lesson you'd like to share during this channeling?

Gabriel: There is nothing, for it is now time to educate yourself by going back and reading all of these channelings. I will communicate with you soon.

Thank you, Gabriel. Take care.

Gabriel: You, too!

Caught you before the hour! How are you, Gabriel?

> **Gabriel:** Somebody's got jokes, I see. Well done, Beau. Well done.

Are you speaking in slang, Gabriel?

> **Gabriel:** I speak in the same language you speak. If I speak similarly to you, then there is a better chance you'll understand me. When I speak to the "All," I use words and language that will make sense to everyone.

Even though everyone speaks differently?

> **Gabriel:** Everyone speaks the same. It just depends on how they were raised and how they decide to speak. Words are words no matter which way you put order to them. The understanding of them will always dominate over how they are communicated.

I don't know how true that actually is. A person may say something with no intention of being mean, but it'll come across as mean and the other person will get offended. I don't see how that works the same way as you just described.

> **Gabriel:** The message is the same no matter how they say it. The person who it's communicated to may take it differently than how it's meant to be spoken. That's a choice.

In other words, someone can say something with no intention of hurting the other person, but the other person may still get offended based on how they decide to hear it at that moment?

Gabriel: You're absolutely getting there. What someone says to somebody is what they say. You can't change that. What you can change is your reaction to it.

(This definitely relates to sarcasm. Someone who doesn't understand sarcasm may take offense at something someone says sarcastically, while someone who does understand sarcasm won't take any offense at it and may possibly even laugh because he understands it was meant in jest.)

That's what I figured you meant. It's the same way with the actions someone will take. We can either be happy about it or upset/mad about it.

Gabriel: It all comes back to choice. Choice is all there is. Things happen, and you get to choose your reaction. Life is not difficult to understand or maneuver through. It may look that way as you go through it; that doesn't mean it is the way you see it. *When you change the way you look at things, the way you look at things changes.*

Isn't that something similar to what Dr. Wayne Dyer says?

Gabriel: It is. I'm glad you caught that.

Is that today's life lesson?

Gabriel: Is it? That's a choice you have to make.

(Here we go again with choice. It's not a bad thing. It's actually kind of comforting to know every single decision we make is a choice. This explains all the bad decisions I've made in the past. Ha!)

How fun . . . Let's make it today's lesson. Please explain this lesson more.

Gabriel: I will do that, for there is a lot to get regarding this lesson. Know that everything I share with you is designed to make you think and to make you aware of what Life is truly all about. How you look at things determines what you see.

The only way to understand this is to think about how you react to situations. Next time a situation happens or someone says something to you, pay attention to how you react and observe the situation. The only thing that differs between a good reaction and bad reaction is how you look at it. Your brain knows how to choose.

It's your ego that makes the decisions, though. If you get angry, take a step back and observe what just happened, reevaluate the situation, and then make your decision. Don't judge any situation or anybody that upsets you without stepping back and taking a breather. Pay attention to the minor details. Pay attention to how *you* react at the beginning. A quick reaction can sometimes be used more to guard and protect yourself than it is to really think.

(What I feel Archangel Gabriel means by that last part is that if something or someone is attacking you, your instincts will immediately guard and protect you to the point you don't really even have time to think about the best option.)

Wow . . . well, that does make sense. In other words, do our best not to have a knee-jerk reaction to things. If something upsets us, take a step back, take a breather, and reevaluate the situation.

Gabriel: I'm glad that you understand that. Pay attention to how you react at first. Be OK with what just happened and then move on. Now, things you consider awful may very well happen, and you are going to react a certain way no matter what in order to protect yourself or a loved one—or you may just break down. I don't expect people to change and think straight when something terrible happens. Do your best to move on. That's all I ask in situations like that. Be the best you.

I'm happy that you said that because what you suggested may not always be doable. There are times we're going to act a certain way no matter how much we know.

Gabriel: And if you do, that is OK.

Thank goodness! Oh, I see what I just did. I responded a certain way based on what you said. I understand it now. I'm happy about that. Is there anything else you'd like to share about this lesson, or is there another lesson you'd like to share?

Gabriel: That is all for today. Thank you, Beau, for giving me the opportunity to communicate through you.

Right back at you, Gabriel! You are a blessing.

Good evening, Gabriel. It's been a busy day, which is why I'm channeling you now. I also understand the idea of priorities.

Gabriel: I'm glad that you understand that idea and concept. It is time to move on from that thought that you did something wrong. Remember the conversations we've had about "right" and "wrong." There is no such thing.

I'd like to discuss words today. Give no power to words, for they are just that: words. Words are not physical entities; therefore, they cannot hurt you. The only thing that can hurt you with regard to words is the meaning you give them. I am sharing this with you because I know you still deal with this with regard to your mom. Your mom says everything with love, but you give her words meaning that is not related to how she intends those words to come across.

This does not mean that nothing she says is coming from a place of frustration, no matter whom she is talking to. She is doing the best she can with the life lessons she has learned throughout her life and the things she's made situations mean. It was her choice to make them mean what she decided, and the same goes for you and your life and everyone else and their life. You are all dealing with being human. You are, as Landmark says, "Meaning-making machines." "X" happens and you make it mean "Y."

That is correct. It's so easy to understand when I hear it like that in plain English. It's harder to deal with in reality, when the situation is happening. How can I remember that formula when things are going awry?

Gabriel: Do you remember a while ago in the last book, I suggested to you to make a list of all the life lessons and keep that list in your pocket? You can do the same thing with these lessons. Again, that is a choice for you to make. You can also just remember the formula "X" happens and you make it mean "Y." It is your decision and your decision only.

Life is a choice at every split second. Yeah, I get that, but again, it's harder to acknowledge it and put it into action while in the moment.

(If everything is a choice, then we are making choices at every single moment of every day throughout our lives. That's nuts. It really reminds you how your choices affect your life. Be wise.)

Gabriel: I shared a lesson with you recently where I told you that when a situation happens and you don't like how it's going, you can take a step back, take a deep breath, and reevaluate the situation.

I remember that well. I will consider making that list of lessons, and even if I don't keep that list in my pocket, I will be able to read it every morning as a reminder. Is there anything else you'd like to share about this lesson, or is there another lesson you'd like to share?

Gabriel: There is nothing else, my child. Be blessed.

You mean to remember I already *am* blessed?

Gabriel: That is correct.

Thank you, Gabriel.

Gabriel, how are you?

Gabriel: I am especially happy to be here with you, for I have a wonderful lesson to share with you that is far and away so much different from anything else I've shared recently.

That is always exciting, and when you say that, it is usually really out there. What is this new lesson?

Gabriel: *The truth of life only lies in your belief.* Let me explain. There is truly no "truth." There is no "lie." There is only Now, and that is all there will ever be. Now is Now is Now is Now is Now. The serendipitous journey you take is only guided by one thing, and that is your spirit. Remember how we spoke about this in more detail during your channeling session with your family friend who also channels me. When life hands you lemons, make lemonade.

Let's take it a step further. When life hands you lemons, make apple juice and then splash it onto yourself. Take advantage of what life gives you, no matter what it is, and then make it something completely different from what you were originally given. Then *own it!* There is only one way to own it, and that is to believe what you've done is the best.

(I don't want to splash apple juice, or any juice for that matter, on me! That would be messy, and I don't want to stain my furniture.)

You said that "the truth of life only lies in your belief." Is that belief the same belief you mentioned earlier, that we should believe what we've done is the best?

Gabriel: The truth lies in what you create, my love. That is all there is to it. Be aware that the ability that you have to be glorious is already within you. You just have to recognize it and realize it is already there.

Is there anything else you'd like to share regarding this lesson?

Gabriel: Design your life however you'd like. Just know that you have the power and ability to make it look *however* you want.

(This is a reminder that we have free will to do what we please. We are also able to shape our life like silly putty. That's awesome! I'm going to shape mine into a motorcycle!)

Got it. Thank you. Is there anything else, or is there another lesson you'd like to share today?

Gabriel: There is nothing else for me to share with you today.

Thank you, Gabriel. Be great.

Gabriel: I will!

What a blessing it is to channel you, Gabriel.

Gabriel: What a blessing it is to have you as a channeler. Be aware that the information that comes through before and during the channeling is me. It can also be your higher Self, but that's more so before I enter. Your higher Self is always speaking to you to guide you in the best direction for you to learn and grow as a human being. There are no limits except for those created in the mind.

Thank you for sharing that. I always figured it was you that was sharing information before I channeled you. It can also be my higher Self, and you're saying more often than not it is?

Gabriel: This is exactly what I am saying.

You told me once that my "everyday angel," Maria, talks to me more often than I realize. I know when she's talking to me because I figure if it's not you, then it's her. But how can I be sure when it's her?

Gabriel: That is for you to figure out. I will give you a hint, though. When you think it is you, it is more than likely her.

(We all have angels around us, and those angels help guide us and communicate through our thoughts.)

That almost makes it sound as if I don't think for myself.

Gabriel: You absolutely do. Your actions are showing that you think for yourself. Remember, it is all a choice. You can be told what the best way to go about things is, and you still make the choice to do what you like. Do you understand this?

I do. That's going to be fun to figure out. It's like a game. That said, what is the next life lesson you can share with me today?

Gabriel: *Your path is chosen for you already, and you change it at any time.*

While I know what you mean by this, the way you say it reads as if we *do* have a predestined path. However, I think you mean that since we are choosing our life moment by moment, we are letting our thoughts, our past, dictate where we go. It can change at any time because we have the free will to do so. Am I correct?

Gabriel: I am happy you understood what I meant. Take into consideration that everything you think about life is incorrect; for example, there is no predestined path—but there is. *You* are the one choosing it. God does not do this. Your thoughts are creating your path. Your past is creating your path. Most people operate from their past. Operate from the future. Operate from what you know yourself to be. There is only the echo of life that flows through you. No path is predestined by God.

(Here's what I feel Archangel Gabriel means by this based on what I've learned in my spiritual studies: We definitely have the free will to take any path we'd like to reach our destiny. If you have a destiny to go to the mall at 2:00 p.m. on Sunday, May 3, 2017, then you will get there on that day at that time. How you get there is your path. It is your free will. Also, what you do there is free will. How you get to the shoe store in the mall that you are destined to be at is done by whatever path you choose to take, and you have the free will to choose it.)

This is a great reminder. Thank you for that.

Gabriel: You have to believe in yourself to create the life you want. You are the painter, and life is the canvas. Your thoughts are the paint.

That's a kickass metaphor! I love that! Is there anything else you'd like to share regarding this lesson, or is there another lesson you'd like to share?

Gabriel: There is nothing else. Take these lessons into your life.

I will. Thank you, Gabriel.

I realized a few minutes ago I hadn't channeled you yet today. I must create structure. It was a busy morning, but I still could have done it after meeting my friend a little after 2:00, instead of letting two hours go by. She challenged me, though! I couldn't pass that up, and I realize that it would have been OK for her to wait thirty-five to forty minutes. Can you suggest anything to help me fix that?

> **Gabriel:** Plan to win all the time and be aware that you may lose sometimes while going through the process. For instance, you *could* have done what your friend asked you to do sooner instead of before the call. I can get into a whole discussion about this, but to put it simply, plan your life. Plan to win and adjust if it looks like you're about to lose so you can continue to win. Plan your days and life to the best of your ability. You are in control. Life will never look how you expected it to look, but it will always look how you planned it when it's all said and done.
>
> The world needs more "doers." It needs more "go-getters." I know we discussed the idea of words like *need,* so I'm saying it in this way, in this context, to get a point across to you. Be a doer. Be a go-getter. You've always wanted to be that, but you've never stepped forward to accomplish it. I love you, Beau. Be great.

(I feel Archangel Gabriel means that even though what the goal we want to see may not look how we pictured it in our mind, the end result will be what we want. While on our journey to get to our goal, we'll realize at times what we thought we originally wanted is not what we really want at all. Therefore, we change it along the way.)

Does that mean I have to give up sleep or at least sleep less than I usually do? I like to get eight hours of sleep, but I usually get between six and seven. I'm still tired in the middle of the day no matter how long I sleep.

> **Gabriel:** What's wrong with taking a nap? It doesn't have to be a long nap. Thirty to forty-five minutes is all you need. Sleep when you can. Your body will let you know when you need to rest. Eat healthily and eat smart. Remember the life lesson I shared with you about doing research? Do that. Do research on foods. Find out your family history. You know what's good for you. Blending is a great way to get a lot of nutrients into one meal, and it doesn't have to be at every meal.
>
> Do your research on what works best for your body and follow that. Experiment with your body. Your guides will never lead you in the wrong direction. If it feels right, then it is right. If it feels wrong, then it won't work for you. Trust your instincts. You know better. You're smart. You're intelligent. You're brilliant. You are a machine. You were built to work at top capacity.

Thanks for being really clear about that, Gabriel. You are hinting to me that we can be our best if we eat cleanly and do our research on what foods work for us and what foods don't.

> **Gabriel:** You understand all of this. Take 100 percent responsibility for your life, Beau. Your life is determined by you and *only* you.

(I'd like to say that through my own research over the years and things I've learned from channeling, a healthy amount of sleep is really important for us to function at our absolute best. I feel that if we sleep well and eat well, we can be at our healthiest. I am no scientist, and I did not go to school for this. This is simply a feeling, and I am also clear that we are all built differently. Do what you feel is right for you and your body. That said, consult with a doctor and nutritionist.)

It all comes back to taking 100 percent responsibility. That means planning ahead as well. We could plan our days, weeks, months, and years in advance. What about the alarms I set for myself in my phone that remind me to start and stop on certain things?

> **Gabriel:** Do what works for you, and remember not to rely on other things to help you achieve your goal. This is in reference to something like an alarm with regard to knowing when to start and stop. Take responsibility and pay attention to the time. That's all there is to it.

What if I wanted to start off with alarms for a couple of weeks and then go off them?

> **Gabriel:** What will that accomplish for you? Don't rely on other people or other things to get you to your goal. I am *not* telling you to do everything yourself. Hold others and hold yourself to account. Be accountable. Be a leader. In fact, you just have to *remember* these things to accomplish them. Remember you already *are* a leader. You just have to be reminded of these things. That's what I am here for—to *remind* you that you already are these life lessons. That's it.

(It is so important to remember that. We don't have to "be" this or "be" that because we already "are" what we want to be. I'm a big believer that the Universe wouldn't put an idea in our mind if it weren't something we could achieve.)

That's all there is to it? You're saying all we have to do is remember who and what we are?

> **Gabriel:** If there were any secret of life, that would be it: *Remember who and what you are.* You are made in the image and likeness of God. God is infinite. God is serendipitous. God is a creator. God does not destroy, though. God will alter things, but God will never

destroy. You can't destroy energy, and if everything is energy, then nothing has ever been destroyed. It has only been changed.

(Remember, everything is energy. You attract what you are energetically.)

Wow . . . Is there anything left to share for this lesson?

Gabriel: This could very well be the end of this book.

Would you like it to be the end of this book?

Gabriel: I'd like you to choose based on your instincts.

(Thanks, Gabriel, for reminding me of the lesson of choice. Ha!)

I feel as if my instincts are telling me I can write more.

Gabriel: You are.

Oh . . . ha, Gabriel! Are there any other lessons you'd like to share for this book?

Gabriel: There is nothing else.

Thank you, Gabriel. Should I continue to channel you every day to start a new book?

Gabriel: Always channel as often as you can, for there is never an end to learning.

Gabriel's Guidance *2*

EXTENSIONS
Love, Karma, and More

Hi there, Gabriel. I got the thought as soon as I closed my eyes to channel you that this would be an extension of Book 2, which I just finished yesterday. I also saw you pull another book out of Book 2 and heard you share that it is an extension during the moment you were about to enter for this channeling. Can you please explain to me what this channeling is based on?

Gabriel: I absolutely will. Hold your horses, for I am going to take you on a journey; this is a communication we haven't dived too much into just yet.

The world is missing a key element to bring peace back to it. That element is love. I want you to get that everything is love. Energy is love. Love is energy. When I tell you that you are an extension of God, you are an extension of love, for love is all there is. It is a love you as a human being can't really wrap your head around. Love is not a noun; love is everything—even an adverb!

The more you know, the less you understand, for the meaning of anything is a choice. Do you understand that all of language is a choice? People made it up. They made certain sounds mean certain things. Even powerful words like *love* and *hate* are just sounds. They are truly expressed through the conviction you give them and how you express them physically in your reality.

Do you understand that all of life is a choice? Do you understand that it is all made up? God does not share things with you in your choice of language. The feelings you get are what form the words. You are still creating words. God does not operate in words. God operates with and communicates with energy. Words have energy, so God is communicating to you through a form of energy. Everything is energy. There is no mistake that the things that are communicated to you are taken out of context. The person a communication comes through is only human and interpreting it how he is choosing to interpret it.

The same goes for you, Beau. Why do you think you are constantly erasing and rewording things? You are interpreting them how you are choosing. It is all a guessing game. You are figuring it out as you go along. This is what new parents do. They are guessing and figuring out how to raise a child. Don't be shaken by the way you do things if they aren't working out how you thought they would. Life—your journey through it—will have hiccups.

That is one of the deepest things you've shared with me so far. I'm really amazed by that. Is there anything else you'd like to share for this extension?

Gabriel: Come back tomorrow and I will share much, much more.

That's so cool. Thank you, Gabriel. I will communicate with you tomorrow.

Gabriel! I am excited to learn what you'll share with me today, considering what you shared with me yesterday. What would you like to share for this extension of Book 2?

Gabriel: Let's talk about karma. Karma is a form of energy that transmutes the circumference of lessons and shares them back with you at a speedy rate. "Do unto others what they do to you" seems to be a regular way of treating others. This is where the "bad" and harmful karma comes into play. I share with you time and time again that life is a choice. I've also shared with you that it is up to you how to treat others, and to treat others with love no matter what is done to you. I'm not saying don't protect yourself. What I am saying is to protect yourself out of love. There is no need to harm to the point of death or to the point of medical care if you truly don't have to. Be your own protector.

Plus, you also have guardian angels. Let them be there for you as well. Learn to protect yourself, though. Learn to be great. The altercations that you face in life are meant for you to blossom. They are meant for you to grow. Things are meant to happen for you to understand certain lessons. Some of those things you may not see as "good" things. That is OK, for you have the ability to make your own decisions. You were given this gift, for this is part of your free will.

(When Archangel Gabriel says, "Karma is a form of energy that transmutes the circumference of lessons and shares them back with you at a speedy rate," I feel he means it goes back to choice. It is our choice how we respond and react to situations, and how *we respond and react defines what our karma and the lessons we'll learn from it look like.*

What Archangel Gabriel says, "Do unto others what they do to you seems to be a regular way of treating others," I think he means that it seems to be normal on our planet to treat others how we treat them. I also know that even when you're kind, some people you interact with have no idea what to do with your kindness and react defensively or angrily. Taking it personally can be a normal way of thinking, but it doesn't solve anything.)

My goodness! I've never heard karma explained in that way. There is so much stuff you share with me to which I can only respond, "Wow! That's amazing," or "Wow! I'm blown away!"

Gabriel: And that is part of your journey. These channelings are not always meant for you to be in conversations with me. Some of these channelings are meant purely for me to share messages with you and everybody who reads them. There is so much more to life than conversation. I really want you to get that. The things that mean the most to you are felt through emotions, and emotions are energy. It's just that simple. That is why I shared what I shared with you during your last channeling. Words are just a form of energy. They are just sounds that were chosen and formed into a language. True communication is expressed through emotions.

Would you say then that the "I have a dream" speech was communicated more through emotion that the words Martin Luther King said?

Gabriel: Recognize that the *only* reason that was so powerful a speech was his conviction when he spoke those words. His words were understood by most, but his conviction was how he expressed his emotion; his emotion is really what made that speech what it was. The message in the words was very important, but if he had given that speech nonchalantly, it may not have had the same impact. Don't think about how he acted outside of that speech. Think about the emotional conviction he put *into* that speech. There is a big difference.

I almost feel like this whole conversation about conviction is geared toward me and how I deliver my lyrics in the music I make.

> **Gabriel:** There is always a connection. Let me share with you how important emotion and conviction are. Blues is felt. It is a form of music that is *felt*. All music that is truly popular [is filled with emotion]. All singers and instrumentalists who are considered great put emotion into their music. Guitarists put emotion into their playing. Singers put emotion into their singing. It is truly that magical gift that makes music great.

This is such a fascinating conversation, and I love that I can really relate to it. It almost feels like it is for me specifically, even though I know it isn't.

> **Gabriel:** You can realize that this will affect everyone who reads it.

Is there anything else you'd like to share in regard to this, or is there another extension you'd like to share with me?

> **Gabriel:** There is nothing, for you need a break from this conversation to let it all soak in. Come back tomorrow, and I will have more to share with you.

OK. Thank you, Gabriel, for sharing all of this.

> **Gabriel:** You are welcome. Remember that you already are perfect in your own way.

I will. Thank you again, Gabriel.

Good morning, Gabriel. How are you this morning?

Gabriel: I am chipper as always!

That's always good to hear. What would you like to share with me today?

Gabriel: The emotional outbursts of laughter that you have are in contrast to the emotional outbursts of tears that you have. Sharing this with you is to talk about the *concept of contrast.* At the beginning of time, there was something created called *duality.* This duality shares its own space in the Universe and shows up to express contrast amongst things. Polar opposites, if you will.

Let us journey a little deeper. With duality comes difference, and with difference could be acceptance. It is a choice to accept. However, it is there; the duality is always there. Where there is black, there is white. Where there is light, there is dark. Where there is "good," there is "bad." This is how the Universe works. This is not just something that human beings on Planet Earth are here to acknowledge. This is a law of the Universe that exists no matter what. You don't have to accept it for it to exist. It exists regardless.

I have found the Law of Duality very intriguing for many years. Can you please explain it in more detail, Gabriel?

Gabriel: This can even be placed in [the context of] what was learned by Einstein: For every action, there is an equal and opposite reaction.

So duality is not just this or that? You are saying that it is the reaction to something happening? I've never looked at it like that.

Gabriel: You will become open to the idea that there is only existence of laws in this Universe and nothing more.

What do you mean by "nothing more"? Actually, I do kind of understand that. Do you mean that there is just "what's so"? Nothing else can exist if it isn't real? If I am right about that, then everything we think of, whether we create it or not, is real.

Gabriel: Manifestation is a law of the Universe. Thought is part of that, so it is also a law. There are laws that haven't been realized just yet either. These laws will be discovered in time.

(Mind. Blown.)

This is really interesting. Is there anything else you'd like to share?

Gabriel: Tomorrow will bring about a new conversation. Be with this for today.

I will. Thank you, Gabriel.

Good morning, Gabriel. It's nice to converse with you this morning and every morning.

Gabriel: Same to you, my beautiful soul. Here is another lesson I would like to share with you. This is perfect, for this extension is actually more of a law than a lesson: *the Law of Gravity*. The Law of Gravity is only recognized as a physical attribute. It is also mental/emotional. When you feel heavy because you have much stress on your shoulders, it will bring you down. When you are light and happy, it lifts you up. When you laugh, it lifts you up. Laughter, just like light, is nearly weightless. When you have so much drama and worry and concern circulating in your space, it weighs you down. You now have all of that weight in the form of stress resting uncomfortably on your shoulders. Be aware that gravity is not just related to things in your physical universe.

(What a fascinating concept! I never considered it was also a law for your mental and emotional state. That takes the Law of Gravity to a whole other level.)

That is such an interesting observation. I wonder how many people look at it that way.

Gabriel: About two thousand people know this lesson, this law. Almost half are people who channel me, and the other half are people who were able to figure it out on their own.

Is there anything else you'd like to share about this lesson/law, or is there another one you'd like to share today?

Gabriel: *The Law of Seismology* is something I'd like to share with you.

I had to look up the definition of *seismology*. It is "the branch of science concerned with earthquakes and related phenomena." Why is this a law, and why are you sharing this with me?

> **Gabriel:** There is a connection here for human beings that has nothing to do with earthquakes but rather with the reaction of how things respond. This is related to the Law of Cause and Effect. When you do something, anything, it causes a ripple effect. This is law and this is nature. When you skip a rock across a pond, the water will start to ripple in the areas [where] it was hit with the rock. Look at the rock as thought. You had a thought, which then skipped across your mind and created visions. Those visions then rippled across the universe. The universe now must mirror those thoughts. You can see your reflection in the water. You are the universe in human form, just like you are water in human form. Remember that you are physically made of more than half water.

(This is boggling my mind even now. These laws are universal, easily explained, and presented in a way that you may never have thought of previously. They go deeper than what is explained in school textbooks. This lesson in particular is life-changing for me. It reminds me how powerful our minds and thoughts really are.)

What a fascinating law! I never ever looked at it like that. Being that seismology is also the branch of science concerned with earthquakes, I guess I can say it is the same idea.

> **Gabriel:** Yes, it is. Be gentle to yourself and others.

I will. Is there anything else you'd like to share with me regarding these lessons?

> **Gabriel:** There is nothing for today.

Thank you so much, Gabriel. This is amazing.

Hi, Gabriel!

Gabriel: Hi, Beau.

What would you like to share with me today?

Gabriel: Everyone has an astrological sign, and that sign can help guide you into what field of work you will be attracted to and do best in. It will help guide you to the kinds of people you will work best with and be in romantic relationships with, if you choose to do so. Remember, you have free will to do whatever you want. You are experiencing life at this moment, and you are your own tour guide. Astrology is a way to help you maneuver best throughout life. It is kind of like a cheat sheet.

(We are our own tour guide, and our astrological sign is our map to follow.)

The way you explain things, especially if those things are what I would consider common knowledge, is always in a different light. They are always talked about in ways I would never have looked at them. Astrology is like a cheat sheet. That's really a unique way to look at it. What else can you share about this?

Gabriel: Know that the road to a successful life can be predicated relatively well if you follow astrology. Follow the laws of your astrological sign, for they will give insight about what will work and what won't work. Now, astrology is not always perfect, for everyone is different and his own individual. But it will still help guide you, for while some people are only partially the definition of their astrological sign, others are exactly the definition of their astrological sign. Even if you are partially that signature, you have the ability to be led in the direction that will work best for you.

Trust your instincts first and foremost. If you read something and it doesn't have any meaning or impact on you, then move on. Follow in your heart what is right and what makes sense.

I guess I will be taking a closer look at my astrological sign!

(You have that right!)

Gabriel: You all come to this earth uninhibited. Be yourself and follow your heart always, in all ways.

Is there anything else you'd like to share about this, or is there anything new?

Gabriel: There is nothing more for today. I love you. Live life fully!

Gabriel, you are so fun to channel. I love you.

Gabriel: I love you too, Beau. How does it get better than this?

Taking phrases I use, huh?

Gabriel: I am speaking to you the same way you speak to others and yourself. It is the same words, or rather as I shared with you recently, the same sounds.

That is correct. So what would you like to share with me today?

Gabriel: There is The Wonderful Life of Beau.

OK . . . what do you mean by this?

Gabriel: *The Wonderful Life of Beau* is the play you have been writing since birth. We talked about this briefly in the last book, and I've discussed this in these new lessons I've been sharing with you. It is called *The Wonderful Life of Beau* because it is specifically about you. If it was about someone named Shelly, then it would be called *The Wonderful Life of Shelly*. Do you understand what I mean by this?

Yes, I do. Would everyone's story start off with *The Wonderful Life of* . . ., even if their life was difficult?

Gabriel: That is fully up to them and how they see their life. If you feel your life is difficult and you constantly express that, then It could very well be named *The Difficult Life of Shelly*.

I like where this is going. Please explain more, Gabriel.

Gabriel: I absolutely will. You are the author, director, and leading actor in your own play. Your play is the life you are living. You can write in situations and characters and practically everything else. You get to write in your scenery, the place you are living in, if you are homeless, if you are sick or have an illness, and everything in between. You can literally write it all out, put those scenes into steps, and watch them unfold. Remember though, that it will never look exactly how you planned, but it will always work out in the way you wanted.

So . . .

Gabriel: God is there to assist in the production. I say this because of what I said before. It may not always look exactly how you pictured it on the way there, and the ending scene may be a little different than how you imagined it. In the end, though, you always get what you envisioned. It may *look* different, but it is always what you wrote.

What about people who come into this world with an illness or disability? They didn't write that in. That's how they were born. Please explain this.

Gabriel: The writing process starts before you ever come to the physical world. Your spirit writes out and decides what kind of life it wants the soul to live. Some people aren't even capable of writing their own play because they are unaware of the fact that they can write it. They just go with the flow. Others are aware enough to change things. It all depends what the soul is here to experience.

That almost seems unfair. That's basically saying that some people have a disadvantage in life *because* they can't write out their life and create what they want due to their disability or illness.

Gabriel: Who said it was a disadvantage? There is no such thing as a "disadvantage." Maybe the point of their life is to just "be." This is what the spirit, the soul, chose for this life. There is absolutely no disadvantage. Disadvantage is an opinion. Disability is an observation. None of them are truth. They are only views.

I feel a saying coming on . . .

Gabriel: You are not someone else's view. What others think of you is none of your business.

This is true. Is there anything else you'd like to share about this lesson, or is there another lesson you'd like to talk about?

Gabriel: There is not. Enjoy your day!

I will. Thank you, Gabriel.

(This has been a great reminder that we control our life. We can create it through writing it or even imagining it in our mind. We are God/the Universe in human form, so we can do anything God/the Universe can do. I don't know about you all, but I'm going to create a milkshake right now.)

Hello, Gabriel. How are you this afternoon?

Gabriel: I am doing incredible, as always. I see you are very tired.

Teddy kept me up most of the night. I'm glad I don't work out today because I could really use the nap time!

(Teddy was the family dog and was very sick at the time of this channel. He is now happily on the other side. I decided to keep this in because it relates to this next lesson.)

Gabriel: This whole thing ties in to the lesson of life for today: *Maintain your well-being.* It is important for you to function at peak performance. Now, I don't want you to think I made your dog keep you up to prove a point, for I did not do that. I see, however, that there is an opportunity to share this message with you based on your current circumstances. Be aware that any time I share something with you, I relate it to something you are currently dealing with. This is a great opportunity to share this.

I'm sure it is. Does maintaining our well-being relate to what you've shared recently about getting the proper amount of sleep for our body, as well as eating in a way to properly maintain top health?

Gabriel: It is all tied together. Be who you want to become. If you want to become someone who is successful in all areas of life, from mind to body to spirit, then yes. Maintain proper well-being.

(I feel that proper well-being is a little different for everyone since we are all individuals.)

I feel like the word *proper* is an opinion, because what is proper to me may not be proper to someone else.

Gabriel: This is correct. What is proper to you is absolutely different compared to someone else. Listen to your body, for your body has all the answers. It always has.

That's so interesting, Gabriel. Is there anything else you'd like to share about this?

Gabriel: There is nothing and there is no new lesson to share for today.

Thank you, Gabriel.

Good morning, Gabriel! How are you this morning?

Gabriel: It's always going to be the same answer, for I am great!

What would you like to share with me today?

Gabriel: I would like to share with you another law of the universe, Beau. This is the *Law of Self-worth.*

There is a law for that? Please explain further.

Gabriel: When you have a large self-worth, the Universe works in conjunction with you at a faster rate. This is related to the concept and Law of Manifestation. They are all connected. To manifest what you want, you must believe that you are willing to accept it and worthy of accepting it. It is that simple. This is where the Law of Self-worth comes in, for you will not attract anything to you that you don't feel you are worthy of having. Do you understand this?

It takes some thinking, but I can get it. To manifest what we want, we must believe and remember that we are worthy of having it.

(There is a difference between self-worth and conceit. You can be very conceited and still not have a great self-worth. Remember, it's not what you display on the outside; it's what you believe on the inside.)

Gabriel: This is correct. Let's say you want a chocolate doughnut. If you don't feel you are worthy of that doughnut, then you will not get it. There is a difference between not feeling worthy enough to have one and not getting one as a result, compared to knowing you're worthy of one and *choosing* not to get one. Do you see the difference?

Yes, because I know I am worthy of a chocolate doughnut right now, and I am choosing not to get in my car and drive to go get one. They aren't healthy. Besides, I had a doughnut a few days ago. I'm good.

(Ba-dum-tshh!)

Gabriel: You're silly. Do you see what I mean, though?

I do understand that. It goes for bigger things, too. If we don't feel like we are worthy of a supermodel boyfriend or girlfriend, then guess what? We aren't going to have one. Is that what you mean?

Gabriel: You understand it well. I am happy about that.

I have always wondered about that, though. There must be some things that we aren't meant to experience or have in this life. I mean this on an individual level. If I can have it all, that means I can become a pilot. However, if I have no desire to *become* a pilot, then I won't have that. What if I wanted to win the lottery when it goes up to ten million dollars? Can I have that?

Gabriel: Thank you for asking about this, for this is where it gets tricky. You can have it all, but that doesn't mean you will be given everything. There is a difference here. For example, you, Beau, would like to have a successful business as a music producer, correct? Well, maybe that's not really meant for you to have. At least not right now or even ever. You see, human beings *want* a lot of things, but remember that if you aren't being given what you want, then either a) you aren't supposed to experience that in this life, or b) God has something even better for you, or c) both. This experience you call "life" isn't always going to give you everything you are striving for.

Now you may still get to where you want, but it may look different from what you envisioned. Don't get caught up in the logistics. Stay focused on the end goal, and things will work out precisely the way they should for you to receive the best outcome.

(As previously discussed, I always wanted a career making hip-hop music. As I became older, I began to move away from that, and now I just want to create music in my own way. I say this because it is what I want, but it's beginning to look totally different from what I previously imagined.)

That explains a lot. Is there anything else you'd like to share about this, or is there a new law or lesson you'd like to share with me today?

Gabriel: The *Law of Gravity!*

What about the Law of Gravity? I thought we already discussed this. Did you want to add something else?

Gabriel: Do you understand that the Law of Gravity is accepted and a lot of these other laws I am sharing aren't? Don't you find that fascinating?

I think it's because the Law of Gravity is not as easily deniable as some of these other laws. A lot of the other laws you've shared with me in this extension of Book 2 I feel are considered a bit "woo-woo." They are a bit "out there" to a lot of people.

Gabriel: Once people realize that there are all these laws, and they understand how they work, the world will shift massively. Patience is a virtue.

I am remaining patient!

Gabriel: I know. Don't give up on humanity.

I'm not. What's going on is scary, and I still have hope.

Gabriel: Don't have hope. Have a knowing. Expect the change. Expect the awakening. Hope carries false pretenses.

(People are still scared almost two and a half years later, at least here in the United States.)

It does, doesn't it? All right, well, if there is nothing else, then it is a good time to end this channeling session. Good-bye, Gabriel. I will communicate with you tomorrow.

Gabriel: Good-bye, Beau.

Good afternoon, Gabriel.

Gabriel: Let's begin a new discussion today. Today I'm sharing with you the *Law of Relativity* in further detail and how it relates to each individual person.

I just found this explanation of it online: "It states that nothing is good or bad, big or small . . . until you *relate* it to something." I love that I found this explanation! We've talked about "good" and "bad" being a choice based on our life experience. What is good to me may be bad to you. This law is really bringing the whole thing full circle. It's going into further detail. How awesome is that?!

Gabriel: It *is* awesome! All of the Universal Laws are awesome. All of the life lessons are awesome. Also remember that *awesome* belongs on the list of words relating to this law. What is awesome to us may not be a big deal to someone else. I personally find everything enchanting because I believe it is. I know it is.

(Is it just me, or does Archangel Gabriel feel everything *is awesome?)*

So what is big to you may be small to me. What's good to you may be bad to me. If I feel someone is mean to me, you may not see it that way. It's all based on our perspective. You just opened up my eyes and reminded me of how I see my mom.

Gabriel: Aren't you getting it now? You observe this world through your own eyes. You are wearing "rose-colored glasses." The most enhanced minds, the most opened minds, aren't wearing glasses. They see things for what they are first and foremost and then choose from there instead of acting based on their past.

(My goodness, that's deep!)

We are protecting ourselves from being hurt.

Gabriel: This is correct, and there is *nothing* wrong with that. All I am here to do is open your eyes and make you realize that there are other ways, less painful ways, easier ways to go about life. Be open to all possibilities.

That seems like it's easier said than done, though. A lot of the lessons you share with me are easier said than done.

Gabriel: And this is why the Law of Relativity exists. You just proved it exists. To you it may seem like a lot of work. To someone else it may seem like common sense.

I see. What else can you share about this law?

Gabriel: The whole Law of Relativity is just a fancy way of saying that we all observe life differently. No two people look at and experience this world identically. There are so many layers to life, and it's your job to peel them away until you realize that everything is connected. You are all the same. We are all the same.

I know that, though.

Gabriel: You understand the concept. You haven't fully grasped the reality of it, though. When you do, you will realize how special you all are.

I just had a little epiphany. This laptop I'm typing on is made of the same "stuff" as I am. Therefore, it is an extension of me. My thoughts are being expressed through this machine, which is part of me. I am forming thoughts into shapes that are recognized as sounds. Some of these thoughts are coming *from* a higher energy. If we are all connected, then you are an extension of me. I am creating this entire conversion, as well as the words that are coming through. This is why you taught me a lesson back in the first book that said, "This is you typing." Since we're all connected and made of the same energy, then yes, it was in fact me typing. I am starting to get all of this at a deeper level.

(This realization proved to me that we are all *the same: you, me, God/the Universe, angels, and energy. This still blows my mind years later rereading it.)*

Gabriel: Yay! I am so happy! Let's go further, shall we? You are making your whole entire world up, literally moment by moment. Nothing really exists. There are observations and a knowing of certain things made by hundreds, thousands, millions, and *billions* of people. They all observe each thing differently. However, that object, that thought, exists because other people also believe it exists and see it with their own eyes—both their physical eyes and their third eye. *Life is made up moment by moment by all living things.* The ones who get this are the ones who are able to create and manifest instantly. You can do this. Please remember that because when you do, you can have it all.

(It's that easy for us to create our life. We say it or write it or both, we visualize it, and then we take action to make it appear.)

I like how you just brought everything back around. I'm blown away right now. Who knew there was so much to life?! You are right about there being layers. This whole discussion boggles my mind, and I am grateful you shared it with me. Thank you. Is there anything else you'd like to share about this law, or this there something new you'd like to discuss?

Gabriel: There is nothing. Let this sink in for today. We will go into further detail about your life tomorrow.

My life? As in me personally?

Gabriel: Yes and no. You'll see what I mean tomorrow.

(Oh boy.)

All right, I guess it's just a waiting game at this point. I will communicate with you tomorrow.

Gabriel: I would like to come in immediately and just tell you that you're creating everything. I won't get into detail because it isn't necessary since you know what I am talking about. I am not mad or yelling at you. I say these thoughts to you with love and *only* love. Just know that you are creating your whole reality: every word, every thought, every scenario. It is all your creation. Do not blame anything else. Any questions or confusion you have are being based on frustration. Take a breather, and take care of what you feel could be done to break the pattern.

Wow . . . Thank you for that, Gabriel. That calmed me down a lot.

Gabriel: We can move on to a beautiful new opportunity of knowledge right here: *God is within you.* We can even say that you are within God.

Well, since we are God in human form, and because we are all One, then I can see how we are in God. God is everything: the universe, water, plants, space, the sun, the moon, the stars, and even energy. Energy is all around us. *We* are energy. That would absolutely have us within God. That's really extraordinary to think about.

Gabriel: Do you want to know what's even more extraordinary? The sun, the moon, and the stars are just extensions of you. Everything is energy, correct? That would mean that those objects are just extensions of you. Human beings are extensions of one another. The laptop you are typing on is an extension of you, as you recognized in a previous channeling session. What's even more extraordinary is that your entire life is created moment by moment simply through thought.

None of this physical world really exists. You are imaging all of this. I shared this with you in greater detail in your channeling session with a family friend recently. The human being you are and the world that you live in are created by your thoughts. There are numerous realities, infinite realities going on in sync with each other, all creating a world that you each experience.

Let's go a little further here. I shared with you that all of your thought is creating your world and that just because someone is blind and cannot see objects does not mean that things don't exist. When there is knowledge of an energetic form, even if only created and made aware by one person, it exists in physical reality. This is why someone who is blind can still bump into a parked car, can still hear things around him, and can still feel the hands of another.

On top of that, if everything is energy, then this is why they can still experience feeling. They can still experience emotions like love, hate, disappointment, and success. Everything is created by the mind, the thought. You as a human being aren't really real. This is all an imaginary world created by your spirit and the spirit is just an extension of God/Energy. You are energy within energy. Know that your life is created by thought and only thought, for you have to think of everything that you do and don't do before you do or don't do it. It is that simple to understand, yet so complex to fully understand within the confines of the human brain.

(That's super deep. This is a good place to take a minute and breathe.)

Where do we even go from here in our discussion?

Gabriel: Who said there was anywhere to go, Beau? "Going" doesn't really exist the same way you think it exists. On the "other side," everything is instant. In your physical reality, things take "time" for almost everybody. Those who have fully mastered the world of manifestation are able to manifest almost instantly.

Don't ever doubt the power you have. Remember what Halley's friend said: The other side, where all the magic is, actually exists here as well. Human beings get caught up in life and forget that the things you get to experience here aren't experienced on the other side. Things like French fries, hamburgers, and candy.

(Halley Elise wrote the foreword to the first book of this series, Gabriel's Guidance.)

Learn to come from a place of gratitude and remember that what you get to experience here is different from what you get to experience when you cross over. Enjoy the opportunities of your physical reality. Don't be afraid of the other side because it is more magnificent than you ever thought it could be. Be excited to cross over when the time comes, but don't try to get there anytime soon. Enjoy your life right now. Enjoy it all the way to the end.

Life is magical. I realize that is easier said than done for a lot of people, but know it is true. Live your life knowing that *you are creating all of it. Just because there are inhumane things happening doesn't mean you have to take part.* You are writing the script of your life through thought. Change your thoughts and you will change your life.

I think this is a great place to end this channeling session. Don't you, Gabriel?

Gabriel: If you choose to do so, then yes, it is a great time. I will communicate with you tomorrow.

Archangel Gabriel, are you there? Is this you?

Gabriel: I am here, Beau. Don't be scared or frustrated or worried about where your life is going, because as long as you write down where you would like to be and envision it through thought, you will get there. The biggest thing you've been dealing with, and why it's taken so long for you to have everything—aside from belief in yourself, which is why I discussed the Law of Self-Worth with you recently—is that you aren't designing a clear path for yourself. You aren't following any kind of map. You aren't planning out your life. You are just letting things happen by circumstance. This may work for some people, and they may be OK with that. It is time to become chipper and to be *excited*.

Is there anything else you'd like to say before we move on to a new law or lesson?

Gabriel: There is nothing! I'm glad to be back! This is so exciting! Let's move on to another law, shall we? Let's dive deeper into these conversations, for there is only you. A new law I can share with you is the *Law of Channeling*. Everyone can channel. Everyone *does* channel. Some channel at different levels. For instance, you channel an archangel. Your friend channels inspiration musically and for his abilities as a mechanical engineer. Another friend channels options for health and strength to use in her own fitness program and teachings of fitness. Photographers channel inspiration for their photos, and so on and so forth.

There is more than one way to skin a cat, as is said. Everyone channels on a different level, and it is only for you to figure out.

Once you figure out what your specialty is, that is what you are the best at channeling. Even intuition is a form of channeling.

Trust your intuition, Beau, for your intuition will always lead you in the direction that will bring you the most success for what you are out to accomplish. The journey of life begins within. Trust in yourself. Know you are worth it and go for it! Love is all there is, and all there is, is love.

Know the divine is there to guide you. It is your ego that will lead you astray. Don't listen to your ego. I am not saying it is an easy task; however, once you realize how to stop listening to your ego and start listening to divine guidance, your life will become a magical forest of wonder and enchantment. There is *nothing* to fear but *fear itself*. The only obstacle course in life is found in your mind. It is found in your thoughts, and you are the only thing that ever stops you. Stop that, for it does not serve you. Life is what you make of it.

(I forgot that we all channel. It's just that each of us channels in a different way from others.)

Everyone channels? I never even looked at it that way. I didn't realize that inspiration was a form of channeling, but now that I know that, it makes perfect sense. Is there anything else you can share about this law?

Gabriel: There is always more to share about each law. I don't share everything all the time, though, because you aren't ready to know all of it just yet. Everything will come out through these channelings. Remember that everything is interconnected. The laws I share with you all share the same message: Trust in the Universe and trust in yourself. Trust, trust, trust.

Well . . . all right! So is there anything else you can share about this law, or is there anything else you'd like to teach me today during this channeling session?

Gabriel: There is one more thing. I want you to remember that I love you for everything you are and everything you are not. Live life and know you are 100 percent responsible for it. There is nothing to fear but fear itself, Beau. Be wise. Better yet, remember that you already *are* wise.

I will. Thank you *so* much, Gabriel. I adore you.

Gabriel: You are here to create, so create the most magical life you can imagine!

Good morning, Gabriel. I am so thankful and glad you came back. I am here to serve you and be the person who channels you for these lessons.

Gabriel: I am glad to be back, for you are so fun to work with. I love your curiosity. Know that the only way for you to grow is to be open to the growth. You have to be ready, and the only way for you to be ready is to be prepared, and the only way for you to be prepared is for you to know you are the chosen one for whatever you are out to accomplish. That may sound religious, but it is not. It is simply a matter of fact that you could be who you want to become and then act *as if*.

You were given an opportunity of a lifetime, and you have to recognize that this was meant for you at this time in your life. This does not make you any more special than anyone else, for you are *all* special. The only thing that ever stops you from being great and being all that you are meant to become is yourself.

I really want to emphasize that. There is no physical being or object that can ever *stop* you from getting to where you want to be. Things may get in the way and become roadblocks, but you have the ability and willpower to figure out how to maneuver around them. Going "straight" is not the only way. In fact, you will almost always have to take detours to get where you want. Life does not work the way you think. The end result you are out to reach is easy to accomplish, but it takes work—hard work. Then again, "hard work" is a matter of opinion. What is hard to you is easy to someone else. Learn to balance life and enjoy the ride.

(Remember that. Hard work is a matter of opinion. What's hard to you is easy to someone else.)

I feel as if the "work" that we all go through on the journey is always "hard." Wouldn't God want to make the journey challenging so we can grow as much as we can? If everything were easy, then there wouldn't be much growth. What can you say about this?

Gabriel: This can go back to the idea and reality of the kinds of lives people are meant to be living during the life they are in. Remember during your channeling session with your family friend that I discussed with you the types of lives there are. There is the "sleeper life," in which the soul lives a life in which everything comes easily. They don't face too many challenges in their life because their soul is on a journey of what many would consider an easy life. This is not a matter of "fair and unfair." This is a matter of growth for the soul. You all experience different things because each soul is different. Know that the only objective for your life is to be the best you can be.

So even when we are living a "sleeper life," as you just said, we should be the best we can be. Even when we live a "hard" life, we should be the best we can be. It doesn't matter what kind of life we are leading, God just wants us to be our best? Is this what you mean?

Gabriel: To an extent, yes, this is what I mean. Let me explain in further detail. The only way for you to grow is to be aware that the life you are living is really happening, and then to just "live." It does not take anything more than breathing to grow. Your soul's experience as a human being is more than enough to grow and learn.

Let's get a little deeper than that. It doesn't even necessarily take breathing to grow. The soul can come into the body while the body is still in the womb and experience growth even if the baby dies before it is born, whether through natural complications or through an abortion. There is absolutely *nothing* sinful about an abortion, for "sin" does not exist. This is something I shared with you in the first book. Since there is no such thing as "good" or "bad," there can be no such thing as "sin." That wouldn't make sense.

What you may consider sinful may not be considered sinful by someone else. *Life is a choice.* Life is an observation. Religion is a matter of opinion. It works for some and doesn't work for others. The beauty of free will is that you get to choose what makes sense to you. There is *nothing* "wrong" with religion. If it works for you, then great! If it doesn't work for you, then great! Do what works for you. Live your life the way you choose to live it, for no one or no thing is judging you.

People may criticize, and the fact is that they aren't judging *you* specifically. They are seeing something in themselves that they don't like and judging themselves while putting the judgment on you. What would your life be like if you didn't take offense at what others thought of you? Remember, what someone thinks about you is *none of your business.* Let them judge. Let them be mad or upset. It is not something you have to worry about, for it is not necessarily affecting you physically. Words are energy. You can choose for them to affect you, or you can deflect them. Most celebrities take words about them to heart, and it affects them mentally and physically. Remember that what others think and say about you is none of your business.

(The whole concept of sin not being real is stated as a matter of fact by Archangel Gabriel, but it is still a matter of opinion as to whether it makes sense in your world.)

I really do my best not to let others' words affect me, but the fact is, a lot of the time they do. I feel like I've gotten better through all the things you've taught me, but I still have a tendency to get upset. It is so much easier said than done.

Gabriel: That is a choice. Do you get that?

Yes, I get that. I don't want to agree with it, and I get it.

Gabriel: I will say it again: What others think about you is *none of your business.*

I got it. Is there anything else you'd like to share regarding this, or is there another lesson or law you'd like to share?

Gabriel: That was a lot for you to take in for a session, so I will end our communication here for today. Take a rest and we will continue tomorrow.

Thank you, Gabriel.

Good morning, Gabriel! You came down and entered while swimming. You might have even been wearing a shark fin and told me you'd explain all of that. What was the reason you swam down?

Gabriel: Everything needs an explanation, doesn't it? You ever wonder why that is so? Let me explain why, if you aren't sure. Human beings are a curious species. Most species are curious. This is just a natural way of being. At no point does the mind say, "Well, I don't really care what they're doing," before it has the thought "Why are they doing that?"

At no point does a plant say to itself, "I wonder if I can reach that height?" It just reaches it. It "goes for the gold." Plants are one of the few species that don't contain the thought process that goes into being curious and wondering if they can or can't accomplish something. They just do.

This is the point I want to make to you. You will always doubt yourself, even if only for a split second, before going on to find out if you can or cannot accomplish a goal. I am here to remind you that you should *never* doubt yourself. There is nothing wrong with curiosity, and there is nothing wrong with doubt. What I am here to remind you is to just go for it. Whatever it is, go for it. Don't ever let fear get in your way to the point it stops you. Use fear as a catalyst to propel you.

Now, let's say you go out and do what you are afraid of and fail to accomplish it. Don't let that get you down. Pat yourself on the back and acknowledge the fact that you made an effort. That in itself is worth being happy about because you conquered your fear even if you didn't accomplish your goal. There is nothing wrong with "failure." There is nothing wrong with making an effort and not reaching a goal. Plus, you may very well have another opportunity to reach it, and if you are lucky enough to have one, then keep going!

(If only I realized this fifteen years ago!)

This is all based around the famous saying you are constantly sharing with me: "There is nothing to fear but fear itself." Is this correct?

> **Gabriel:** That is correct, Beau. Do you realize that all of these things I've been sharing with you can relate directly to your own life? I mean that literally, as well as for others. These lessons can and will make a difference in your life specifically, Beau, if you choose to take them *into* your life. That is a choice.

One of my friends touched on that yesterday. I have to go back and reread all of this.

> **Gabriel:** And I keep telling you to do that. You seem to be brushing it off, though.

I never realized that you were talking to me directly with all of this knowledge and referring to my own life. I get that this is for everyone, and I guess you've been focusing on sharing things that relate directly to me. That's phenomenal. Why are you doing that?

> **Gabriel:** I am coming through *you* for these channelings. I want *you* to be as powerful as you can because of that. Beau, I don't ever want you or anyone else ever to doubt your or their power. It's that simple. You are infinite beings living in a finite world. I am here to help you be as infinite as possible. There are no mistakes made in the Universe. The Universe is perfect, for God is perfect and you are the perfect You. Please understand this message if no other. You were born to be amazing, so no matter what, you are.

This information is really blowing my mind. Where do we go from here in this conversation?

Gabriel: There is nowhere else to go, for this will end the expansion of Book 2. You may take a break from channeling me for a few days. Use this weekend to read over these expansions and then come back to me for Book 3, for I will bring with me other energies to share information about the Universe, which we haven't talked about just yet.

(Another book?! Awesome!)

Wow! That is so exciting! I am looking forward to Book 3 and to see what new energies come through! I am smiling ear to ear.

Gabriel: That's awesome. Be great, Beau, for you are amazing. Until next time, stay well.

ACKOWLEDGMENTS

Ani, you have made me a better person and always supported me in my spiritual growth. I love you purely.

Mom, you have been a huge supporter of my channels and cheered me on all the way. I love you so much and thank you.

Shirley, thank you for your continued love and acceptance. I love you.

ABOUT BEAU BUTGER

Beau Butger was born in the heart of New York City. Just before his fourth birthday, he and his parents moved to South Florida and have stayed there ever since.

Beau developed his creative instincts through his love of music and design. He has been writing and producing hip-hop music for over twenty years and had a career as a graphic designer for eight years.

Around 2006, not realizing he was being guided by something greater, he dove into the study of spirituality and swallowed up everything he found. Then, around 2012, his whole world changed when he became conscious that he was a channel for Archangel Gabriel, who is known to work with artists and writers.

Since then, he has channeled many other energies and expanded his creative endeavors, including the release with this book of two published books. It has led him down a path he never looked for, and he couldn't feel more fulfilled.

For more information, please visit **www.beaubutger.com**